I Ching Explained

I Ching Overview, History, Fundamental Concepts,

Step by Step Guide for Consulting, Hexagrams and More!

By Riley Star

Copyrights and Trademarks

All rights reserved. No part of this book may be reproduced or transformed in any form or by any means, graphic, electronic, or mechanical, including photocopying, recording, taping, or by any information storage retrieval system, without the written permission of the author.

This publication is Copyright ©2019 NRB Publishing, an imprint. Nevada. All products, graphics, publications, software and services mentioned and recommended in this publication are protected by trademarks. In such instance, all trademarks & copyright belong to the respective owners. For information consult www.NRBpublishing.com

Disclaimer and Legal Notice

This product is not legal, medical, or accounting advice and should not be interpreted in that manner. You need to do your own due-diligence to determine if the content of this product is right for you. While every attempt has been made to verify the information shared in this publication, neither the author, neither publisher, nor the affiliates assume any responsibility for errors, omissions or contrary interpretation of the subject matter herein. Any perceived slights to any specific person(s) or organization(s) are purely unintentional.

We have no control over the nature, content and availability of the web sites listed in this book. The inclusion of any web site links does not necessarily imply a recommendation or endorse the views expressed within them. We take no responsibility for, and will not be liable for, the websites being temporarily unavailable or being removed from the internet.

The accuracy and completeness of information provided herein and opinions stated herein are not guaranteed or warranted to produce any particular results, and the advice and strategies, contained herein may not be suitable for every individual. Neither the author nor the publisher shall be liable for any loss incurred as a consequence of the use and application, directly or indirectly, of any information presented in this work. This publication is designed to provide information in regard to the subject matter covered.

Neither the author nor the publisher assume any responsibility for any errors or omissions, nor do they represent or warrant that the ideas, information, actions, plans, suggestions contained in this book is in all cases accurate. It is the reader's responsibility to find advice before putting anything written in this book into practice. The information in this book is not intended to serve as legal, medical, or accounting advice.

Foreword

Divination is the process of reading or interpreting signs or symbols with the intention of receiving guidance for a person's current situation and/ or to somehow foresee what the future brings. The various divination systems began during the ancient times and continued through the Middle Ages, and surprisingly some of it is still being used in today's modern world.

One of the classic ancient systems of divination that stood the test of time and had been around for a thousand years is called I Ching or the Book of Changes. It originated in China, and it is undoubtedly the oldest and most important books in world literature. It has become the pillar of historical, philosophical, and spiritual values especially for Chinese scholars and gurus during the ancient times. The text of I Ching contains more than 2 millennia of commentaries and interpretations making it an influential text that can be used in various fields including arts, literature, religion, business, and psycho – analysis. It has also become a significant tool for westerners in understanding eastern philosophy.

The I Ching is now being used symbolically to guide a person especially when it comes to moral values and decision making; this is why it's no surprise that the two main branches of Chinese philosophy which is Taoism and Confucianism has its roots from this ancient divination system.

Table of Contents

Introduction to I Ching 7

Chapter One: What is the Book of Changes? 2

    The History of I Ching 4

    The Eight Trigrams and their Attributes 8

Chapter Two: The Book of Wisdom 10

    The First Fundamental Concept: The Yin and Yang 12

    The Second Fundamental Concept: The Theory of Ideas 14

    The Third Fundamental Concept: The Judgements 16

Chapter Three: Consulting I Ching for Your Daily Life 18

    Posing the Correct Question 19

    The I Ching's Answer 20

Chapter Four: Step by Step Guide on How to Use I Ching . 24

    How to Use the I Ching 25

Chapter Five: Hexagrams 1 to 10 30

Chapter Six: Hexagrams 11 to 20 50

Chapter Seven: Hexagrams 21 to 30 68

Chapter Eight: Hexagrams 31 to 40 86

Chapter Nine: Hexagrams 41 to 50 106

Chapter Ten: Hexagrams 51 to 64 126

    Conclusion 150

Photo Credits 152

References 154

Introduction to I Ching

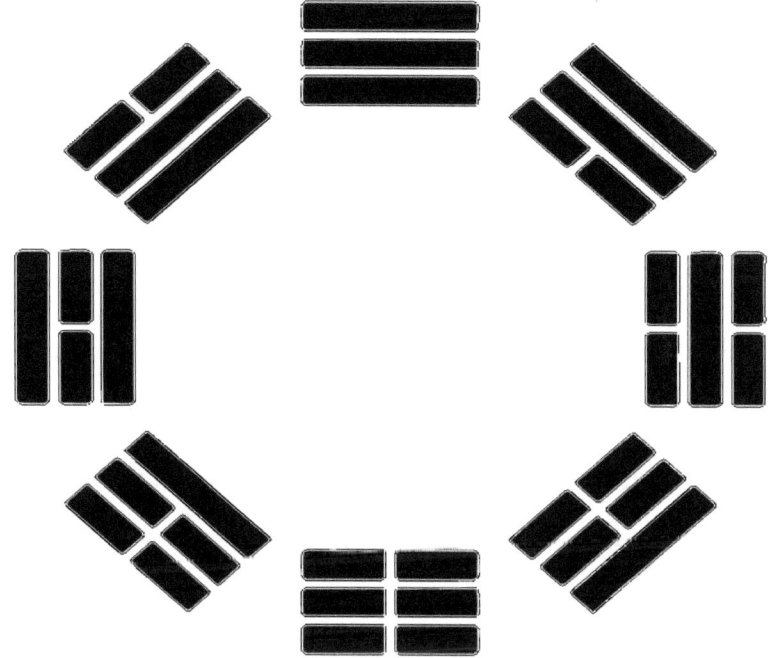

I Ching is the Chinese word or translation of the Book of Changes. It is undoubtedly one of the classic and most important books in history; the origin of I Ching dates back to the ancient times and has mythical roots. The Book of Changes has occupied the attention of the greatest minds of China up to the present day, and almost all of the greatest and most significant in the 3,000 years of Chinese literature and cultural history was either inspired, influenced, or based

Introduction to I Ching

from the interpretation of the book. Therefore it is safe to say that I Ching contains the wisdom of a thousand years! In fact, the two main branches of Chinese philosophy which is the Taoism and Confucianism both have their common roots in the Book of Changes.

I Ching sheds new light on the many and usually puzzling thoughts of Lao – tse (a mysterious wise figure), and his students. Axioms of Confucianism were accepted back then without further confirmation but through I Ching one can understand and interpret it better.

The wisdom of I Ching doesn't only encompass Chinese philosophy because the statecraft and the field of science have never ceased to draw inspiration and guidance from the Book of Changes. Among all the Confucian classic literature, I Ching survived the burning of books during the reign of tyrant Ch'in Shih Huang Ti.

The teachings of I Ching is a way of life for the Chinese, and its influence transcends in Chinese culture. If

Introduction to I Ching

you are to go through the streets of China, you will find that it is saturated with the influences of I Ching. For instance, you'll find a fortune teller that's ready to draw from the ancient book in order to guide her and give appropriate counsel to the minor perplexities in his/ her subject's life. You'll also find that lots of wooden panels in people's houses which are done in gold on black lacquer are sometimes covered with inscriptions of quotations from the Book of Changes to remind and counsel people especially during difficult times.

I Ching had become the pillar of Chinese philosophy which is why in the course of time, various occult philosophies or doctrines that are completely irrelevant to it has come to be linked with the book's teachings even if some have not originated in China. The Han and Ch'in dynasties witnessed the start of a more formal natural philosophy that seek out to embrace life's perplexities and thought through a system of numeric symbols. It is combined with the famous doctrine of two worlds – the Yin and Yang with the "five stages of change" doctrine which was taken from the Book

Introduction to I Ching

of History – and because of this, it forced the philosophical thinking of Chinese intellectuals to a more rigid formalization which increasingly made the Book of Changes appear to be seen as a cabalistic speculation and something that's really 'mysterious.' Some people thought that I Ching is profound but unfathomable because the past and future was forced into a numerical system. Such speculations during the time of Mo Ti and his students are to be blame because the seeds of a free Chinese natural science were destroyed and was instead replaced by a sterile tradition of reading and writing literature. This is perhaps the reason why China became an image of hopeless stagnation especially in the eyes of the Westerners.

Apart from the mechanistic number mysticism, one should not overlook the fact that there is a living stream of deep wisdom from a thousand years that is constantly flowing into the book which can be applied into people's everyday lives. China's great civilization highly benefited from the collections of wisdom by various scholars throughout the ages leaving the remnants of the last indigenous culture.

Introduction to I Ching

So what is the Book of Changes? For you to gain understanding about its teachings and philosophies, you should first boldly remove the dense overgrowth of interpretations that has turned into irrelevant ideas. This is essential whether you are dealing with mysteries and superstitions of old Chinese magicians or the theories of European scholars today who try to explain all historical cultures in terms of their experience of primitive savages. You must hold to the fundamental concept that I Ching should be interpreted in the era where it belongs and in the light of the book's own content. And with this, the unclear will perceptibly lighten up as you begin to understand its teachings just like any other classic books that have come down since the ancient times to the modern era we have today.

Introduction to I Ching

Chapter One: What is the Book of Changes?

In Chinese literature, the Book of Changes or I Ching is authored by four teachers namely, Confucius, Fu Hsi, the Duke of Chou, and King Wên.

Fu Hsi is one of the earliest legendary figures in China; he is known as the creator of the linear symbols of I Ching or the Book of Changes during the period when men is still hunting and fishing for a living. This means that the signs or meaning are so ancient that it occurred before any historical memory. Furthermore, the 8 trigrams have names

Chapter One: What is the Book of Changes?

that aren't linked to any forms of Chinese language, and because of this people thought that the names originated from a foreign language. The trigrams are not also identified as archaic characters even if some people thought that it has some kind of resemblance among ancient Chinese characters.

The 8 trigrams are found to be occurring in different combinations during the early times. Two book collections that are considered as a relic are namely, the Book of Changes of the Hsia dynasty known as the Lien Shan, and the Book of Changes of the Shang dynasty known as Kuei Ts'ang.

The Lien Shan is said to have begun with the hexagram Kên (Keeping Still), and the Kuei Ts'ang began with the hexagram called K'un (The Receptive). According to historians, they cannot tell whether the names of the 64 hexagrams being followed today are used back then, and if so, whether they are the same structure that's now present in the I Ching or Book of Changes.

Chapter One: What is the Book of Changes?

The History of I Ching

According to tradition, the 64 hexagrams that are being used today have originated from King Wên who is the predecessor of the Chou dynasty. According to history, King Wên may have added a few interpretations to the hexagrams while he was in prison during the time of a tyrant named Chou Hsin. The text pertains to the individual lines that came from his son who is the Duke of Chou. This form of book entitled the Changes of Chou (Chou I) was used as an oracle during the whole Chou dynasty, and it has been proven from a number of ancient historical documents. This was the status of the Book of Changes before Confucius came upon it. It was believed that in his old age, Confucius made some changes and carefully studied it, which is why historians believe that the T'uan Chuan (Commentary on the Decision) was his work. The Commentary on the Images also traced indirectly to him. There was also a third treatise wherein there's a detailed commentary on the individual lines of the hexagram, and are thought of to be very valuable; it was compiled by Confucius' students and perhaps successors. However, only fragments of it survived.

Chapter One: What is the Book of Changes?

One of the principal followers of Confucius named Pu Shang is believed to be the one who spread the knowledge about the Book of Changes. With the development of speculations in the philosophical value of the book as reflected in Chung Yung (Doctrine of the Mean), and Ta Hsüeh (Great Learning), this type of philosophy created an ever increasing influence upon I Ching's interpretations. A literature called Ten Wings contains fragments of I Ching that dates back to very ancient time, and some from a later period. The main difference can be found not just in the content but also in its intrinsic value.

The Book of Changes escaped the fate of being burned and gone forever. During the time of the tyrant Ch'in Shih Huang Ti many classic books were ordered to be burned. Hence, if there's anything in the legend that burning alone is the reason why many of the classic books were mutilated forever, the Book of Changes should at least be intact; however, this is not the case because in reality it is the collapse of ancient cultures as well as the changes in the writing systems caused damages suffered by all ancient literature.

Chapter One: What is the Book of Changes?

After I Ching had become firmly established as a book of magic and divination during Ch'in Shih Huang Ti time, the fang shih or school of magicians during the Ch'in and Han dynasties made it their prey. Historians believe that the Yin and Yang doctrine were introduced through the work of Tsou Yen which was later spread out by ancient figures like Tung Liu Hsiang, Chung Shu, and Liu Hsin.

The task of editing the book of all its rubbish was Wang Pi's job; he was a wise scholar who clarified the meaning of I Ching as being a book of wisdom and not a book of magic and divination. He soon found emulation and the doctrine of Yin and Yang which was being taught in the school of magic were eventually displaced due to the statecraft philosophy that was slowly developing.

During the Sung period, the Book of Changes was used as a basis for the *t'ai chi t'u* doctrine which was believed to not have come from China. The commentary provided by the elder Ch'êng Tzú's had started the custom of separating the old commentaries found in the book of Ten Wings and instead place them with each of the hexagrams they pertain to. Thus I Ching became some form of a

Chapter One: What is the Book of Changes?

textbook that relates statecraft and life philosophies. After awhile, Chu His rehash the Book of Changes as the book of oracles; he published commentaries on the I Ching and also provided introductions concerning the art of divination.

The critical – historical school of the last dynasty took I Ching in hand but they were less successful in interpreting the Book of Changes compared to other classics because they oppose the Sung scholars and their preference for the Han commentators who at the time are already nearly done in compiling the Book of Changes.

The Han commentators were influenced by theories of magic, then during the K'ang His era, a good edition of I Ching or the Book of Changes were published entitled Chou I Chê Chung. The Chou I Chê Chung presented texts and wings on a separate form but it includes the best commentaries of all periods. This is the basis of I Ching's edition that we use today.

Chapter One: What is the Book of Changes?

The Eight Trigrams and their Attributes

Symbol	Name	Attribute	Image	Family Relationship
Ch'ien	the Creative	strong	heaven	father
K'un	the Receptive	devoted, yielding	earth	mother
Chên	the Arousing	inciting, movement	thunder	first son
K'an	the Abysmal	dangerous	water	second son
Kên	Keeping Still	resting	mountain	third son
	the Gentle	penetrating	wind, wood	first daughter

I Ching Explained

Chapter One: What is the Book of Changes?

Sun				
☲ Li	the Clinging	light-giving	fire	second daughter
☱ Tui	the Joyous	joyful	lake	third daughter

Chapter Two: The Book of Wisdom

The Book of Changes has far greater significance and has other uses as being the book of wisdom. Lao - tse used The Book of Changes as a book of wisdom, and it is believed that some of his profoundest philosophies were inspired by it. This is the same thing with Chinese philosopher Confucius; he devoted himself to reflect and learn from The Book of Changes, and he imparted the wisdom he learned to his students in oral teaching. The version of The Book of Changes that we now have today was annotated and interpreted by Confucius himself.

Chapter Two: The Book of Wisdom

If you take a look at the philosophy permeates the book, it is confined to important and basic concepts. The underlying idea of the whole idea of The Book of Changes or the book of wisdom is simply change. Confucius compared change with the river, he said: "Everything flows on and on like this river, without pause, day and night." When one perceives the real meaning of change; one is no longer fixated on the transition of it but instead upon the eternal law at work or the process of the change itself. This is also Lao – tse's law which is known as the tao or t'ai chi – the principle of the one in the many.

According to Lao – tse, the great primal beginning of all that exists and the fundamental assumption is change. Other Chinese philosophers devoted their thought to the idea of the great primal beginning; a still earlier beginning known as wu chi, was represented by the symbol of a circle. The t'ai chi was symbolized by this circle which is divided into two – the light and the dark – also famously known in the east as the Yin and the Yang.

Chapter Two: The Book of Wisdom
The First Fundamental Concept: The Yin and Yang

The Yin and Yang symbol has become a significant principle especially in India as well as in Europe. However, the gnostic – dualistic concept are not align to the original idea of the I Ching because what Yin and Yang suggests is simply the ridgepole (t'ai chi) or the line. The line represents oneness, duality comes into the world, and the line creates a world of opposites (an above and below; forward and backward; right and left etc.)

The duality concept of the Yin and Yang became popular especially during the transition period of the Ch'in and Han dynasties in China; these dynasties were the time period before our era. It was the time when every student or person carries the doctrine of Yin and Yang. It became the notion, and it became a very important principle to live by.

At the time, the Book of Changes or I Ching was use as a book of magic; the students read concepts that are not originally in the book. The Yin and Yang doctrine has naturally attracted the attention of foreigners outside of

Chapter Two: The Book of Wisdom

China since the primal principles it that of a male and female (duality).

Some philosophers compared the Yin concept as "the overcast" or "the cloudy" while the Yang is a "banner that's waving in the sun," "bright," "shining." The duality concepts were also explained as the dark and light sides of a river or a mountain. In the case of a mountain, the southern part is the brighter side while the northern area is the darker side. Similarly, in the case of the river, if it was seen from a bird's point – of – view, the southern side is in the shadow (yin), while the northern side where the light is being reflected is the bright side (yang). The duality concepts were carried over to the Book of Changes, and were applied to the two alternating primal states of being. It's important to note though that the Yin and Yang don't occur in such derived sense either in the old commentaries or in the actual book itself.

The dual concept first occurred in the Great Commentary, which already shows influence from Taoism. In the Commentary on the Decision, yin and yang weren't used instead it was referred to as "the yielding," and "the firm" respectively. Do take note that whatever terms are applied to these dual concepts, it is certain that the world of being arises out of interplay. Thus change is conceived as a continuous transformation of a force into the other and also as a cycle of phenomena where they themselves are connected such as summer and winter, day and night. Therefore, change is not meaningless; it is subject to tao or the universal law.

The Second Fundamental Concept: The Theory of Ideas

The second fundamental concept in the Book of Changes is its theory of ideas. The 8 trigrams are images that aren't so much of objects as of states of changes. This view is linked with the concepts that Lao – tse and Confucius taught to their students in their oral teachings – that every manifestation in the visible and physical world is the effect of an "image," vision or an idea of the unseen world or spiritual realm. Accordingly, everything that happens in our world is only a reproduction or perhaps a reflection of the events that we perceive or expect it to be which is beyond our sense of perception.

Chapter Two: The Book of Wisdom

The holy men and sages who are aligned or who can communicate with such higher realms or levels of the unseen world gain access to ideas through using their intuition making them able to intervene or decisively take part in the manifestation of events in the world. Thus man is linked with heaven and with the earth - the world of ideas and the material world form a trinity of primal powers.

The theory of seen and unseen ideas is applied in a twofold sense; the I Ching shows the image of events as well as the unfolding of the conditions. If one will discern and reflect upon it to create a better decision in the present moment, one must learn to foresee the future and to also understand the past. In this way, the images or symbolism on which the hexagrams are based will serve as the pattern for what one should do in a certain situation. The Great Commentary doesn't only adapt the course of nature that's made possible but it also attempts to trace the origin of all the inventions and practices of mankind to archetypal ideas and images. Even if the hypothesis can or cannot be applied to specific circumstances, it still contains a certain truth.

Chapter Two: The Book of Wisdom

The Third Fundamental Concept: The Judgements

The third element that's fundamental to the Book of Changes is the judgments. The judgments interpret the images in the hexagram, and it indicates whether a given action will bring fortune or misfortune as well as humiliation or remorse. The judgments help a man when it comes to making a decision to desist from a course of action that's indicated by the circumstance of the moment but could not be beneficial or perilous in the long term. In this way, one makes himself independent of the tyranny of situations. The judgments and interpretations open to the readers and students the richest treasure of Chinese wisdom. A person can have a comprehensive knowledge and view of human experience through it as this can enable a person to shape his/ her life according to his own will and accord it or align it with the ultimate universal law of tao.

Chapter Two: The Book of Wisdom

Chapter Three: Consulting I Ching for Your Daily Life

The I Ching's ethical and intellectual guidance can be unlocked through a general perusal of the texts within each chapter. A person can also consult and seek guidance from the I Ching to provide answers to personal questions or bring a person closer to the truth that he/ she is trying to find. Since I Ching is a book of universal wisdom, it will always give the seeker appropriate answers provided that one follows the rules dictated by the book's structure. In order for a seeker to effectively use the I Ching as a guide to

Chapter Three: Consulting I Ching for Your Daily Life

answer specific questions, one must learn to adapt the question to the structure established by the book which is the Yin and Yang doctrine. The book will only answer questions in a dualistic approach wherein there will be two alternatives and each one requires a different action.

It's important to note that when a seeker is consulting the I Ching for answers or guidance, the seeker should only create a question that are answerable by the two paths or possibilities since it follows the Yin and Yang doctrine. If used properly, the I Ching will offer concrete answers to the right questions, and it will always lead the seeker to the right course of action.

Posing the Correct Question

For instance, you are facing with the dilemma of accepting a job offer in another country which could mean that you need to decide whether or not you'd be willing to leave your home. If you ask it in this way: "Should I accept the job offer in another country or should I just stay in my

Chapter Three: Consulting I Ching for Your Daily Life

home country?" The I Ching won't yield you an answer. You must formulate the question in these ways:

- "Should I accept the job offer in another country?" or,
- "Should I stay in my home country?"

As you can see, if you formulate the question this way, the I Ching can ultimately guide you and provide an answer because it's answerable by either a negative or a positive which is what the Yin and Yang doctrine is all about.

The I Ching's Answer

The I Ching's answer to the properly formulated question aforementioned may warn you that at the moment, you lack the needed endurance or experience to undertake a specific path, and that it would be risky to embark on a particular course without first acquiring more experience or building strength. By illuminating the outcome of every foreseeable situation, the Book of Changes will guide a person to become mindful of the steps that one must take

Chapter Three: Consulting I Ching for Your Daily Life

before doing anything or acting in a particular path. It will also guide a seeker on how to undertake and successful complete a specific endeavor so that even if there are difficulties or obstructions along the way, the action that one will take remains favorable.

The I Ching's astonishingly accurate answers to people's queries are not a mystery because the book is based on the principle of objectivity. Usually when a person is facing hardships and have no clue on what to do, they seek a trustworthy person or perhaps a trusted confidant to ask for advice; this could be a friend, mentor, parent, leader etc. People generally tend to do that because one's subjectivity doesn't allow a person to view a problem with a clear mind, and this is usually because our emotions are entangled with the problem which is why it obscures reality.

Whenever we explain a certain problem to a trustworthy confidant, usually two operative factors happen that makes a person arrive towards a possible solution; first, we must clearly explain the problem and provide elaborate details as well as the possible outcomes thereby further

Chapter Three: Consulting I Ching for Your Daily Life

clarifying the conflict for ourselves. Second, that person will now consider the problem from another angle and can therefore provide perhaps a more objective opinion. The combination of the clear explanation and the objective opinion of your trustworthy confidant may help resolve the problem but keep in mind that even if we seek guidance or advice from others, the answer is already within us it's just that most times we don't have a clear mind to be able to 'see' it.

If you start to see the problem in a more objective way, you can then start to open up and accept external guidance that will help and lead you in finding the right answers or taking the right course.

The I Ching answers a seeker's question in a similar manner. When a person learns how to externalize the problem in a form of question, the I Ching will make you better understand your situation, and you'll be able to accept the logic behind I Ching's answer. If you accept it, you can be guided accordingly. The gift of I Ching is that it helps people to view their circumstances with objectivity so that one can take the right action to achieve a desired outcome.

Chapter Three: Consulting I Ching for Your Daily Life

You can choose to consult the I Ching as a general book of wisdom or you can also use it to seek guidance through posing the appropriate question and answer system that is align with how the book is structured. In either case, you'll learn from its images, and you'll be guided by the principles and ethics which will further enrich your life and elevate you as a human being who can be of better service to your society

Chapter Four: Step by Step Guide on How to Use I Ching

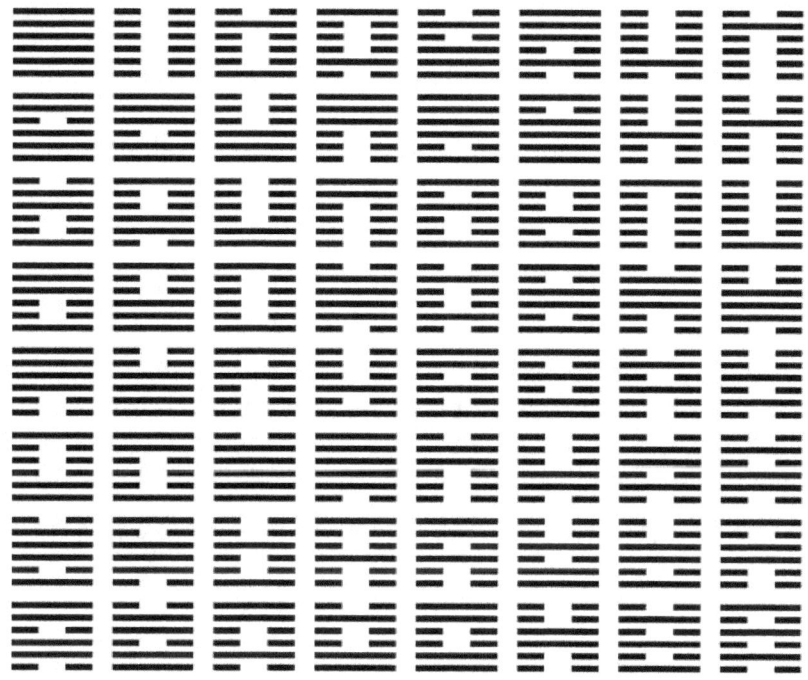

The I Ching has 64 interpretations for each hexagram and lines. The one that is most used is the I Ching that provides 64 short stories which is quite difficult to understand. The metaphoric nature of the short stories you'll find in the next chapters will require expertise and practice. If you aren't sure what it meant by it, ask for guidance from someone who has experience in interpreting each hexagram.

Chapter Four: Step by Step Guide on How to Use I Ching

How to Use the I Ching

Step 1: Question and Answer

As mentioned in the previous chapter, the question you should ask should be something that is currently pre-occupying your mind, and must not be answerable by a simple yes or no. Some suggests that the timeframe to your question should be over the next few weeks or months (short to mid – term).

In the next few chapters, you will get to know the meaning of each hexagram. The hexagram will answer the question and also give advice. First, it will tell a person if the goal that one wants to achieve is favorable or not. Second, it will guide a person on what course of action or what kind of path will one experience as he/she accomplishes a goal. And finally, if there are any challenges that stand in the way of success, I Ching will give an advice on how to modify or overcome such barrier in order for the intended outcome to be successful or at least create a manageable risk.

Chapter Four: Step by Step Guide on How to Use I Ching

Step 2: Toss the coins six times

The next step is to toss your 'lucky' coins. You must have three coins that are sentimental or significant to you. If you don't have that kind of coin, some people purchase online but they buy something that matches their profile. For instance, you can buy a coin that has your birthday number on it or wedding anniversary date etc. You can also buy ordinary coins and just meditate on them.

What you should do is to toss your coins six times while you're thinking about your question. Make sure to have a paper or notebook with you because you need to record the pattern of the heads/ tails according to the key below; the pattern of lines should go from bottom to top in your record just like this:

--------- X --------- = 6th/final toss; 3 tails

----------O--------- = 5th toss; 3 heads

--------- . --------- = 4th toss; 1 tail, 2 heads

--------- . --------- = 3rd toss; 1 tail, 2 heads

-------------------- = 2nd toss; 2 tails, 1 head

-------------------- = 1st toss; 2 tails, 1 head

Chapter Four: Step by Step Guide on How to Use I Ching

- This gives you a hexagram or 6 – line patterns.

- You can also cut the hexagram in half to yield two trigrams or 3 - line patterns: an *upper* (4th through 6th toss) and *lower* (1st through 3rd toss).

- If there are any changing signs, this could mean that there are two readings; the first tells you how things are at the present while the second tell you how it will be after the period of flux are done.

Step 3: Get numbered readings

Check if the result has any changing signs; for instance if you tossed 3 heads or 3 tails. If there is, that means you have 2 readings.

For the interpretation of 2 readings, you need to break up your resulting hexagram into 2 trigrams lower trigram is your first 3 coin toss; upper trigram is your last 3 coin toss.

Chapter Four: Step by Step Guide on How to Use I Ching

Step 4: Interpreting the Meaning of Each Line

Just like any other ancient divination system, I Ching has a set of rules for accurate interpretation. In order for you to fully understand each hexagram, take a look at what aspect of your life each line represents:

- Line one: This reveals the basic issue of your question.

- Line two: This answers what is currently changing about your circumstances, and whether or not your problem/ query can be supported.

- Line three: This pertains to the things or factors that can affect your situation intrinsically (strength, weakness, barriers etc.) that you need to overcome to get desirable or favorable results.

- Line four: This reveals other people's influence over your situation, and it also refers to how the first 3 lines combine in order to influence this line's position.

Chapter Four: Step by Step Guide on How to Use I Ching

- Line five: This answers the unforeseen situations or life events that can either change your current circumstance or reveals to you what is controlling a particular situation.

- Line six: This pertains to your situation not being balanced or in harmony because there's either too much yang or yin energy. It may advise you on how you can rectify your situation.

Chapter Five: Hexagrams 1 to 10

Hexagram 1: The Khien Hexagram

Image: Heaven above, Heaven below.

Attribute: Yielding

    The universe is united and powerful. This is too for a wise man who knows how to execute his action using his creativity and power. Progress comes by applying persistence.

Chapter Five: Hexagrams 1 to 10

- The 1st (lowest nine), undivided: The dragon which represents the subject is lying in the deep and is hidden. This denotes that it's not the time for any active endeavors or doing.

- The 2nd nine, undivided: The dragon which represents the subject is appearing in the field. This denotes that it'll be an advantage to meet with a great man.

- The 3rd nine, undivided: The superior man is vigilant and also active all day. In the evening he is apprehensive and quite careful. It is in a dangerous position but there'll be no mistake.

- The 4th nine, undivided: The dragon which represents the subject is seen as if he is leaping but still in the deep. There'll be no mistake.

- The 5th nine, undivided: The dragon which represents the subject is on the wing in the sky. This denotes that it'll be an advantage to meet with a great man.

- The 6th (uppermost nine), undivided: The dragon which represents the subject is exceeding the proper limits. This denotes that repentance could happen.

- The lines of this hexagram are undivided and strong. If the host of dragons learns divest themselves, this can denote good fortune.

Hexagram 2: The Khwan Hexagram
Image: Earth above, Earth below.
Attribute: Yielding

The receptive earth is power. The wise man learns to follow the natural path of calmness and also correct form of persistence. This can denote that others may lead while you are supporting their aspirations.

- The 1st six divided: The subject is treading on hoarfrost. This denotes that a strong ice will come by and by.

Chapter Five: Hexagrams 1 to 10

- The 2nd six, divided: It represents the attributes or characteristics of being square, great, and straight. Operation without repeated efforts can be at an advantage in every respect.

- The 3rd six, divided: This denotes that the subject is keeping his excellence under restraint but he is also firmly maintain it. He may occasionally engage in service but he won't claim the credit for himself.

- The 4th six, divided: The symbol is a sack that's tied up. This denotes that there'll be no ground for praise or blame.

- The 5th six, divided: The symbol the yellow lower garment. This denotes that there'll be massive good fortune.

- The 6th six, divided: The symbol shows a dragon fighting in the wild. The blood is purple and yellow.

- The lines of this hexagram are divided and weak as what appears from the use of number six. If the subject is continuously correct and firm, it could be advantageous for them.

Hexagram 3: The Kun Hexagram
Image: Water above, Thunder below.
Attribute: Confusion.

The thunderclouds denote a profound disquiet. One must undertake no distant aim but organize support. One must concern itself with only the problems of the moment.

- The 1st nine, undivided: The symbol shows the subject has difficulty in advancing. It'll be an advantage if the subject is firm. One can also be made as a feudal ruler.

- The 2nd six, divided: The symbol shows that the subject is obliged to return or is in distress. The horses of one's chariot may also seem to be retreating. One will continue to seek a wife but the lady will decline a

Chapter Five: Hexagrams 1 to 10

union and maintain her firm correctness. After 10 years, she will accept union and bear children.

- The 3rd six, divided: The symbol is following a deer without the guidance of an expert forester, one may find himself lost in the middle of the forest. The superior man that's acquainted with risks will think that it'll be better to give up the chase. If he went forward, he might regret it.

- The 4th six, divided: Denotes that a lady will seek the help of a man who is to be his husband. Advance will be fortunate and advantageous.

- The 5th nine, undivided: It denotes that there could be difficulties when it comes to dispensing the rich favors that is expected from the subject but with firmness, there'll be good fortune in small things.

- The 6th (uppermost six), divided: The symbol shows that the subject is with his horses and its chariot is obliged to make a retreat. It denotes that there could be sacrifices as the symbol also denotes weeping tears of blood in the streams.

Hexagram 4: The Mang Hexagram
Image: Mountain above, Water below.
Attribute: Inexperience.

As spring water collects at the base of a quiet mountain so does a person becomes enlightened and increases his level of understanding through learning about persistence and decisiveness.

- The 1st six, divided: The symbol shows respect to the dispelling of ignorance. One could take advantage to use such punishment for a certain purpose to be able to remove the shackles from one's mind. Going towards the way of punishment will make one experience an occasional regret.

- The 2nd nine, undivided: The symbol shows that the subject is exercising patience with the ignorant and this could bring good fortune. If one admits the goodness of women, it can also bring fortune. The subject may also be described as a son who's able to sustain his family's burden.

- The 3rd six, divided: The symbol may advise that a man shouldn't marry a woman who only see a man for his wealth for it will not bring any advantage.

- The 4th six, divided: The symbol shows that the subject is bound to be in the chains of ignorance and there'll be occasional regrets.

- The 5th six, divided: The symbol shows that the subject is one without experience.

- The 6th (uppermost nine), undivided: The symbol shows that one is smiting a young and ignorant person but no benefit will come from harming the young ignorant.

Chapter Five: Hexagrams 1 to 10

Hexagram 5: The Hsu Hexagram

Image: Water above, Heaven below.

Attribute: Waiting.

Don't be worrisome. One must wait with confidence. The desired moment will arrive when one knows how to become properly persistent as this will bring progress.

- The 1st nine, undivided: The symbol shows that the subject is waiting in the distant border. The best thing to do is to constantly maintain his purpose for in which case there'll be no error.

- The 2nd nine, undivided: The symbol shows that the subject is waiting on the sand of the mountain stream. One will suffer from other people who will speak against him but in the end one will receive good fortune.

- The 3rd nine, undivided: The symbol shows the subject in the mud which is in close proximity to the stream. One is thereby inviting harm or injury.

Chapter Five: Hexagrams 1 to 10

- The 4th six, divided: The symbol shows that the subject is waiting in the place where there is blood though he will be triumphant in getting out of this unfortunate place or situation.

- The 5th nine, undivided: The symbol shows that the subject is waiting amidst a feast; with such firmness one will receive good fortune.

- The 6th (uppermost six), divided: The symbol shows that the subject has entered an unfortunate situation but three guests will come to help him to get out. If the subject receives the guests with respect, good fortune will happen to him in the end.

Chapter Five: Hexagrams 1 to 10

Hexagram 6: The Sung Hexagram

Image: Heaven above, Water below.

Attribute: Conflict.

This represents heaven and water, strength and profundity as well as conflict. One must avoid confrontation and yield with caution. One must not persist against challenges.

- The 1st six, divided: The symbol shows that the subject is not perpetuating the matter about which there is contention. Others will speak against him but in the end will be fortunate.

- The 2nd nine, undivided: The symbol shows that the subject is unequal to the contention. If one retires and keep concealed, he will not fall into any mistake.

- The 3rd six, divided: The symbol shows the subject in keeping in the old place assigned for his support. The position is potentially dangerous but good fortune is

Chapter Five: Hexagrams 1 to 10

waiting at the end. Should the subject do something for another person, he will not take credit from it.

- The 4th nine, undivided: The symbol shows that the subject is unequal to the contention. The subject will return to studying ordinances and changes, and he will rest in being correct and firm. There'll be good fortune in the end.

- The 5th nine, undivided: The symbol shows that the subject contends with good fortune.

- The (uppermost nine), undivided: The symbol shows how a subject may have the leathern that's conferred on hum, and thrice it will be taken from the subject one day.

Hexagram 7: The Sze Hexagram

Image: Earth above, Water below.

Attribute: Cooperation

The receptive earth holds the water. The wise one will find strength in the company of many friends. Proper leadership will bring forth good fortune and persistence.

- The 1st six, divided: The symbol shows that the host goes according to the rules. If the rules are not good, it will bring forth evil.

- The 2nd nine, undivided: The symbol shows that the leader is in the midst of the host. This will bring good fortune and no mistakes.

- The 3rd six, divided: The symbol shows that the host have many inefficient leaders. There'll be evil if this is the case.

- The 4th six, divided: The symbol shows that the host is in retreat. There'll be no mistake.

- The 5th six, divided: The symbol shows that there are birds in the fields. This denotes that any seizing or destruction will be at an advantage. There'll be no error. If the oldest son leads the host, but the younger men idly occupy what is assigned to them, even if the oldest son may properly lead, there'll be evil.

- The (uppermost six), divided: The symbol shows the great ruler delivering his charges. He will appoint some to rule other states while others will undertake the leadership of clans.

Hexagram 8: The Pi Hexagram
Image: Water above, Earth below.
Attribute: Unity

The receptive earth below with the water above denotes that there's a need for collective awareness and unity to achieve a common goal. One should not procrastinate. One should cooperate with others and return to the plan.

Chapter Five: Hexagrams 1 to 10

- The 1st six, divided: The symbol shows that the subject is trying to seek out sincerity in order to win an attachment. There'll be no mistake. One should be full of sincerity because at the end it will bring other benefits.

- The 2nd six, divided: There is a movement towards attachment and union inwardly or towards the mind. If one practice correctness, there'll be good fortune.

- The 3rd six, divided: The symbol shows that the subject is seeking for union with such as ought not to be associated with.

- The 4th six, divided: The symbol shows that the subject is seeking for union with someone that's beyond himself. Good fortune is sure to come if done with correctness.

- The 5th nine, undivided: The symbol shows that one affords the most illustrious instance of finding attachment and union.

- The (uppermost six), divided: We see one seeking union without sincerity, there'll be evil.

Hexagram 9: The Hsaio Khu Hexagram
Image: Wind above, Heaven below.
Attribute: Restraint.

The winds of gradual change supported by the strength of Heaven denote that restraint will bring contentment and progress. One should make minor changes and conceal all actions.

- The 1st nine, undivided: The symbol shows that the subject is pursuing his own course and returning. There'll be good fortune.

- The 2nd nine, undivided: The symbol shows that the subject returns to his proper course. There'll be good fortune.

Chapter Five: Hexagrams 1 to 10

- The 3rd nine, undivided: The symbol suggests the idea of a carriage where the strap has been removed. It also shows a married couple looking on each other but their eyes are averted.

- The 4th six, divided: The symbol shows that the subject possess sincerity. Any potential danger is warded off and any ground for apprehension dismissed. There'll be no error.

- The 5th nine, undivided: The symbol shows that the subject possesses sincerity while attracting others to be one with him. One is rich in resources, and he employs his neighbors.

- The (uppermost nine), undivided: Shows how the rain or problems has fallen, and how it brought about progress. One should value the lessons of the virtues.

Hexagram 10: The Li Hexagram

Image: Heaven above, Lake below.

Attribute: Correct conduct.

The excessive is beneath, and the strong is above. One must discriminate between the superior and inferior in order to achieve progress. One must remember that change gives way to stability.

- The 1st nine, undivided: The symbol shows that the subject is treading an accustomed path. There'll be no error, if one goes forward.

- The 2nd nine, undivided: The symbol shows that the subject is easy. It also symbolizes a solitary man and if he maintains his correctness, he will receive good fortune.

- The 3rd six, divided: The symbol shows a one – eyed man who thinks that he can see. It also shows a lame man who thinks he can walk. This indicates ill fortune.

Chapter Five: Hexagrams 1 to 10

- The 4th nine, undivided: The symbol shows that the subject is treading on the tail of a tiger. If the subject takes caution, there'll be good fortune in the end.

- The 5th nine, undivided: The symbol shows the resolute tread of its subject. Even if the subject is correct and firm, there will be danger.

- The (uppermost nine), undivided: It denotes that one should look at the whole course that one has trodden. If one learns to examine the omens, and that the course is complete and has no error then there'll be good fortune

Chapter Five: Hexagrams 1 to 10

Chapter Six: Hexagrams 11 to 20

Hexagram 11: The Thai Hexagram

Image: Earth above, Heaven below

Attribute: Prosperity.

The strength of Heaven surrounds the receptive earth. A wise man or leader will surely benefit from this harmony. Good fortune will come.

- The 1st nine, undivided: The symbol suggests that a grass is being pulled up and it brings with it other stalks whose roots are connected. Any advance will be lucky or fortunate.

- The 2nd nine, undivided: The symbol shows that the one who can bear with the uncultivated, and doesn't forget the distant will prove that one is acting in accordance with his course.

- The 3rd nine, undivided: The symbol shows that even if there's no state of peace, one is not liable to be disturbed. If one is firm and correct any distress or problems that will arise will not affect him. The happiness felt in the present will be long enjoyed.

- The 4th six, divided: The symbol suggests that the subject is fluttering down. One will ask help from his neighbors, and his neighbors will come with the sincerity of their hearts to help.

- The 5th six, divided: The symbol denotes that any marriage undertaken is bound for happiness and there'll also be great fortune.

- The 6th six, divided: The symbol shows that the city wall returned into the moat but it is not time to use the army for no matter how firm or correct one is, it will cause regret.

Hexagram 12: The Phi Hexagram
Image: Heaven above, Earth below.
Attribute: Stagnation.

The strong one and the receptive one don't see eye to eye. Strong people will give way to the inferior while the enlightened one will remain reserved in order to avoid any misfortune. There'll be no advantage in persistence.

- The 1st six, divided: The symbol suggests that a grass is being pulled up and it brings with it other stalks whose roots are connected. If the subject shows

Chapter Six: Hexagrams 11 to 20

firmness and correctness, there'll be progress and good fortune ahead.

- The 2nd six, divided: The symbol shows that the subject is obedient and patient. If an average man behave or accord himself, there'll be good fortune. If a great man accord himself as the obstruction and distress require, he will be successful.

- The 3rd six, divided: The symbol shows that its subject is ashamed of the purpose folded

- The 4th nine, undivided: The symbol shows that the subject is in accordance with the ordination of Heaven thus commit no mistake. His friends will come and share in his happiness.

- The 5th nine, undivided: The symbol shows that we see one who brings distress and obstructions to a close.

- The 6th nine, undivided: The symbol shows that there's a removal of obstruction and distress. Hereafter there'll be nothing but happiness.

Hexagram 13: The Thung Zan Hexagram
Image: Heaven above, Fire below.
Attribute: Community.

Strength of Heaven, dependence of fire; this denotes that one recognizes the dependence of their colleagues and companions. A wise person will seek the collective flow in order to gain advantage.

- The 1st nine, undivided: The symbol shows the representative of the union of men or an organization. There'll be no error.

- The 2nd six, divided: The symbol shows the representative of the union of men that's in relation with his relatives; there'll be occasional regret.

Chapter Six: Hexagrams 11 to 20

- The 3rd nine, undivided: The symbol shows that the subject has hidden his arms in the thick grass and is located in the top of a high mound but for 3 years he makes no demonstration.

- The 4th nine, undivided: The symbol shows that the subject is mounted on the city wall, but doesn't proceed to make an attack for he learns how to contemplate. There'll be good fortune.

- The 5th nine, undivided: The symbol shows the representative of men's union wails and cries then laughs. His great host conquers and they meet together.

- The (uppermost) nine, undivided: The symbol shows that the representative of men's union met in the suburbs but there'll be no occasion for repentance.

Chapter Six: Hexagrams 11 to 20

Hexagram 14: The Ta Yu Hexagram

Image: Fire above, Heaven below.

Attribute: Sovereignty.

The strength of heaven holds intelligence which is the maker of an enlightened leader. One must learn how to resist evil and exalt good. Correct leadership will bring great progress.

- The 1st nine, undivided: The symbol suggest that there should be a realization of both the danger and difficulty of a position so that there'll be no mistake to the end.

- The 2nd nine, undivided: The symbol shows a large wagon with a load. One who advances in any direction will commit no mistake.

- The 3rd nine, undivided: The symbol shows that a prince presents his gifts to the Son of Heaven; an

Chapter Six: Hexagrams 11 to 20

ordinary man would be unequal to such an obligation.

- The 4th nine, undivided: The symbol shows that the subject learns to keep his resources under restraint. There'll be no mistake.

- The 5th six, divided: The symbol shows there is sincerity in the subject and it is reciprocated to others that are represented in the hexagram. When one displays proper majesty, there'll be good fortune.

- The (uppermost) nine, undivided: The symbol shows that the subject is given guidance from Heaven. There'll be advantage in every respect and also good fortune.

Hexagram 15: The Khien Hexagram
Image: Earth above, Mountain below.
Attribute: Moderation.

The tranquil mountain in the middle of a receptive earth denotes great progress through the reduction of an excess. Progress will come by equality of extremes.

- The 1st six, divided: The symbol shows us that a superior man adds humility to humility. If one does this, there'll be great fortune.

- The 2nd six, divided: The symbol shows us humility has made itself recognized, and if there's correctness there'll be great fortune.

- The 3rd nine, undivided: The symbol shows that a superior man that has an acknowledged merit will maintain success and also have great fortune.

- The 4th six, divided: The symbol shows a person that is advantageous in every respect and as a result the more he will become humble.

- The 5th six, divided: The symbol shows the one without being rich is able to help his neighbors. All of his movements will be advantageous.

- The 6th six, divided: The symbol shows us that humility has made itself recognized.

Hexagram 16: The Yu Hexagram
Image: Thunder above, Earth below.
Attribute: Harmony

From the receptive earth comes a loud thunder; the wise gains advantage through the harmony of his supporters.

- The 1st six, divided: The symbol shows the subject proclaiming his contentment and pleasure. There'll be evil

Chapter Six: Hexagrams 11 to 20

- The 2nd six, divided: The symbol shows that one is firm as a rock. One sees a thing without waiting until it has come to pass; with firmness there'll be good fortune.

- The 3rd six, divided: The symbol shows one looking up to get favors while he indulges the feeling of contentment and pleasure. However, if he is late in doing so, there could be repentance.

- The 4th nine, divided: The symbol shows one from whom the contentment and harmony comes. One will obtain great success and if he doesn't allow any suspicions to enter his mind, companions will be drawn to him.

- The 5th six, divided: The symbol shows one with chronic complains but who lives on without dying.

- The (uppermost) six, divided: The symbol shows a subject with a darkened mind that's devoted to the satisfaction and pleasure of the time but if one change his course there'll be no error.

Hexagram 17: The Sui Hexagram
Image: Lake above, Thunder below.
Attribute: Flexibility.

Growth and persistence still produces progress even in the midst of excess. An enlightened person leads and also adapts the way from darkness to light or comfort.

- The 1st nine, undivided: The symbol shows that one is changing the object of his pursuit but if one is correct and firm there'll be good fortune.

- The 2nd six, divided: The symbol shows us a person who adheres closely to the little boy, and learns to let go the old man with experience.

- The 3rd six, divided: The symbol shows one adheres closely to the man with experience and age, and learns to let go of the little boy. If so, one will get what he seeks but he will benefit more if he adheres to what is correct and firm.

- The 4th nine, undivided: The symbol shows that one follows and obtains adherents, even he is correct and firm, there'll be evil.

- The 5th nine, divided: The symbol shows us that the leader who is sincere in fostering everyone that's excellent will have good fortune.

- The (uppermost) six, divided: The symbol shows that sincerity is firmly held and bounds fast.

Hexagram 18: The Ku Hexagram
Image: Mountain above, Wind below.
Attribute: Repair.

Winds of gradual change wear away the mountain which denotes that one should learn how to cultivate action in

Chapter Six: Hexagrams 11 to 20

others in order to bring about repair and progress. If one is just starting, one must meditate on the future.

- The 1st six, divided: The symbol shows that a son is dealing with the problems caused by his father. If the son is able, then the father will escape the blame of committing the error. The position is dangerous but good fortune will come in the end.

- The 2nd nine, undivided: The symbol shows a son dealing with the problems caused by his mother. He should not carry his firm correctness.

- The 3rd nine, undivided: The symbol shows a son dealing with problems caused by his father. There could be an occasion for repentance but there'll be no great mistake.

- The 4th six, divided: The symbol shows a son viewing indulgently the problems caused by his father. If he go forward, the son may find a cause to regret it.

- The 5th six, divided: The symbol shows a son dealing with the problems caused by his father. The son will obtain the praise of using the fit instrument for his work.

- The 6th nine, undivided: The symbol shows that one who doesn't serve either a feudal lord or a king but one prefers to attend to his own affairs.

Hexagram 19: The Lin Hexagram
Image: Earth above, Lake below
Attribute: Promotion.

The earth above reflects the lake beneath; so is the enlightened one who is willing to teach and learn from other people. Progress will come if one is persistent.

- The 1st nine, undivided: The symbol shows that the subject is advancing with the company of others, and through one's firm correctness comes great fortune.

Chapter Six: Hexagrams 11 to 20

- The 2nd nine, undivided: The symbol shows that the subject is advancing with the company of others; there'll be good fortune. One will be advantageous in every respect.

- The 3rd six, divided: The symbol shows that one is well - pleased to advance but one's action will not be advantageous. If one becomes anxious about the move, there'll be no mistake.

- The 4th six, divided: The symbol shows one advancing in the highest mode; there'll be no mistake.

- The 5th six, divided: The symbol shows the advance of wisdom such that fits a leader or ruler; there'll be good fortune.

- The 6th six, divided: The symbol shows the advance of generosity and honesty; there'll be good fortune and commit no mistake.

Hexagram 20: The Kwan Hexagram

Image: Wind above, Earth below

Attribute: Contemplation

As the winds moves over the earth, so too the leaders of old travelled the world, contemplated various cultures and visited different regions. It denotes that one should explore new ideas.

- The 1st six, divided: The symbol shows an image of a lad which cannot be blamed by men who are inferior in rank but is a matter of regret for superior men.

- The 2nd six, divided: The symbol shows a person peeping out from a door. It'll be more advantageous if it were the firm correctness of females.

- The 3rd six, divided: The symbol shows that one is looking at the course or path of his own life; deciding if one should advance or recede accordingly.

Chapter Six: Hexagrams 11 to 20

- The 4th six, divided: The symbol shows one contemplating the glory of the kingdom. It'll be advantageous if one seeks to be a guest of the king.

- The 5th nine, undivided: The symbol shows that one's companion is contemplating his own course. A superior man will not fall into any mistake.

- The 6th nine, undivided: The symbol shows one's companion contemplating his character to see if he is indeed a great man; one will not commit error.

Chapter Seven: Hexagrams 21 to 30

Hexagram 21: The Shih Ho Hexagram

Image: Fire above, Thunder below.

Attribute: Reform.

The lightning and thunder's turbulence denotes that something needs to change. One can achieve progress through reform, and one should also administer justice.

- The 1st nine, undivided: The symbol shows that one has his feet in the stocks, and he is deprived of his toes. There'll be no mistake.

- The 2nd six, divided: The symbol shows one biting through the soft flesh and is about to bite his nose. There'll be no error.

- The 3rd six, divided: The symbol shows that one is gnawing with dried flesh, and will meet with something that is disagreeable. There'll be no error but only a small regret.

- The 4th nine, divided: The symbol shows one gnawing the flesh dried on the bone, and also getting the pledges of arrows and money. It'll be beneficial to him if he realizes the difficulty of the task but remains firm in which case, there'll be good fortune.

- The 5th six, divided: The symbol shows one gnawing at dried flesh, and finding yellow gold. One must be firm and correct as the position is quite perilous. There'll be no error.

- The 6th nine, undivided: The symbol shows that one is wearing the cangue, and is deprived of his ears. There'll be evil.

Hexagram 22: The Pi Hexagram
Image: Mountain above, Fire below.
Attribute: Serenity.

Illumination shows the foot of an immovable mountain; a wise man perceives and knows how to avoid disputes. There'll be no progress except in small matters.

- The 1st nine, undivided: The symbol shows that one is adorning his feet. One can discard a carriage and can walk barefoot.

- The 2nd six, divided: The symbol shows one is adorning his beard.

Chapter Seven: Hexagrams 21 to 30

- The 3rd nine, undivided: The symbol shows that the subject appears to be adorned with rich favors. He must sustain his firm correctness for there'll be good fortune.

- The 4th six, divided: The symbol shows one appearing as if he was adorned, but only in white. It depicts as if one is mounted on a white horse while intervening not as a robber; there's intent on matrimonial alliance.

- The 5th six, divided: The symbol shows one is adorned by his occupants. He may look stingy but there'll be good fortune in the end.

- The 6th nine, undivided: The symbol shows one with white as his ornament. There'll be no mistake.

Hexagram 23: The Po Hexagram

Image: Mountain above, Earth below.

Attribute: Deterioration.

The weak earth can't support the mountain; the realm deteriorates. One who is enlightened stabilizes their lives through being generous towards the needy.

- The 1st six, divided: The symbol shows that one is overturning on the couch because of his injured legs. The injury will cause destruction of one's firm correctness, and there'll be evil.

- The 2nd six, divided: The symbol shows one is overthrowing the couch by destroying its frame. The injury will cause destruction of one's firm correctness, and there'll be evil.

- The 3rd six, divided: The symbol shows that the subject is among those who will overthrow but there'll be no error.

- The 4th six, divided: The symbol shows that one's subject has overthrown the couch, and will harm anyone who is lying in it. There'll be evil.

- The 5th six, divided: The symbol shows that the subject is leading others just like a string of fishes. There'll be advantage in every respect.

- The (uppermost) nine, undivided: The symbol shows the subject as a great fruit that hasn't been eaten yet. The superior man will find his people as a chariot carrying him while the ordinary men will overthrow their own dwellings.

Hexagram 24: The Fu Hexagram
Image: Earth above, Thunder below.
Attribute: Repetition.

The start of a new cycle shows that repetition will bring new progress toward a certain aim. Friends will return, and the repeating cycle is part of the Way.

Chapter Seven: Hexagrams 21 to 30

- The 1st nine, undivided: The symbol shows that its subject returns from a mistake of no great extent and won't need or require repentance; there'll be good fortune.

- The 2nd six, divided: The symbol shows that one's admirable subject returns; there'll be good fortune.

- The 3rd six, divided: The symbol shows that one has made repeated returns. There is danger in this position but there'll be no error.

- The 4th six, divided: The symbol shows one's subject moving right to the center yet returning alone in his correct path.

- The 5th six, divided: The symbol shows the noble return of the subject. No repentance is required.

- The (uppermost) six, divided: The symbol shows the subjects are all astray to return. There'll be evil. There'll be calamities and great defeat. The defeat will extend for ten years, and the ruler of the state will not be able to repair the catastrophe.

Hexagram 25: The Wu Wang Hexagram
Image: Heaven above, Thunder below.
Attribute: Spontaneity.

The strength above and the activity below denote an alignment to a natural state. One must act with inspiration and persistence but without a true aim.

- The 1st nine, undivided: The symbol shows that its subject is free from insincerity. One's advance is accompanied with good fortune.

- The 2nd six, divided: The symbol shows that the one who reaps without having ploughed, and gathers the produce of his 3rd year's fields without cultivating them during the 1st year will be an advantage in any direction one desires.

Chapter Seven: Hexagrams 21 to 30

- The 3rd six, divided: The symbol shows that a calamity happens to the one who's free from insincerity. A passer – by will find him and will carry him off.

- The 4th nine, undivided: The symbol shows a case wherein if a subject can sustain its firmness and correctness, there'll be no error.

- The 5th nine, undivided: The symbol shows the one who is free from insincerity but he has fallen ill. Let him not use medicine for the journey to his recovery has occasional joy.

- The (uppermost) nine, undivided: The symbol shows the one who is free from insincerity will also fall into error, and if he takes action, he'll not be advantageous in any way.

Hexagram 26: The Ta Khu Hexagram

Image: Mountain above, Heaven below.

Attribute: Potential.

The strength of the Heavens below comes from within the mountain; the enlightened one studies his past to gain wisdom and develop one's own character.

- The 1st nine, undivided: The symbol shows that its subject is in a dangerous position. It'll be beneficial if he will stop any of his advancements.

- The 2nd nine, undivided: The symbol shows that the strap of a carriage is removed.

- The 3rd nine, undivided: The symbol shows one's subject urging his way with good horses. It'll be beneficial if one realizes the difficulty of this path, and to be firm and correct one must exercise himself on his methods of defense on a daily basis so that he'll be advantageous in whatever direction he may advance.

- The 4th six, divided: The symbol shows a young bull having the piece of wood over his horns; there'll be a good fortune.

- The 5th six, divided: The symbol shows the teeth of a castrated hog; there'll be good fortune.

- The (uppermost) nine, undivided: The symbol shows one's subject is in command of heaven's firmament; there'll be progress.

Hexagram 27: The I Hexagram
Image: Mountain above, Thunder below.
Attribute: Nurturing

The energy stirs under immobility; one must be cautious in expression, and he should avoid negativity. Persistence will likely bring good fortune.

- The 1st nine, undivided: appears to be thus addressed, 'You leave your efficacious tortoise, and look at me till your lower jaw hangs down.' There'll be evil.

- The 2nd six, divided: The symbol shows one is looking downwards for nourishment which is contrary to what is correct, or if one is seeking it from above. If one advances it will lead to evil.

- The 3rd six, divided: The symbol shows one's acting is contrary to the nourishing method. However, firm one is, there'll be evil. One should not take any action for ten years for it will not be advantageous in any way.

- The 4th six, divided: The symbol shows one that is looking downwards for nourishment. There'll be good fortune and he will not fall into any error.

- The 5th six, divided: The symbol shows one acting contrary to what is proper and consistent; if one remains firm, there'll be good fortune.

- The 6th nine, undivided: The symbol shows from who comes the nourishing. The position is dangerous but there'll be good fortune.

Hexagram 28: The Ta Kwo Hexagram
Image: Lake above, Wind below.
Attribute: Imminent change.

The enlightened one withdraws from the world to progress towards one's own goals; stress is imminent.

- The 1st six, divided: The symbol shows that one is placing mats in the white grass for the things that's set on the ground. There'll be no mistake.

- The 2nd nine, undivided: The symbol shows a decayed willow that's producing shoots as well as an old husband with a young wife. There'll be an advantage in every respect.

- The 3rd nine, undivided: The symbol shows a beam that is weak; there'll be evil.

- The 4th nine, undivided: The symbol shows a beam that's curving upwards; there'll be good fortune.

- The 5th nine, undivided: The symbol shows a decayed willow that's producing flowers as well as an old wife in possession of a young husband. There'll be no occasions of praising or blaming

- The (uppermost) six, divided: The symbol shows the subject with extraordinary courage that's wading through a stream until the water hides the crown that's in his head. There could be evil but there are no grounds for blame.

Hexagram 29: The Khan Hexagram
Image: Water above, Water below.
Attribute: Danger.

Being profound will produce difficulties. A wise man learns to become confident because of perils. One must remain calm and should keep all his actions virtuous.

Chapter Seven: Hexagrams 21 to 30

- The 1st six, divided: The symbol shows that one's subject is in a double defile yet he is entering a cave within it; there'll be evil.

- The 2nd nine, undivided: The symbol shows the subject in all dangers of the defile. He will get a small amount of deliverance that he is seeking.

- The 3rd six, divided: The symbol shows that the subject whether he descends or ascends will be confronted by a defile. All is danger to him for his endeavors will lead him into the pit. No action is necessary in such a case.

- The 4th six, divided: The symbol shows that one introduces his important lessons as his ruler's intelligence admits; there'll be no error in the end.

- The 5th nine, undivided: The symbol shows the water of the defile that's not yet full but order will be come forth soon; there'll be no error.

- The (uppermost) six, divided: The symbol shows that its subject is bound with cords of 3 strands, and is placed in thickets of thorns but in 3 years he will not learn the proper path that he must pursue; there'll be evil.

Hexagram 30: The Li Hexagram
Image: Fire above, Fire below.
Attribute: Enlightened intelligence.

Intelligence shines above and below; an enlightened man gains progress through cultivating his intelligence and persistence. One must align itself with goals that bring enlightenment.

- The 1st nine, undivided: The symbol shows that one is ready to move even with confused steps, but he treads reverently; there'll be no mistake.

- The 2nd six, divided: The symbol shows the subject in his place in yellow. This denotes good fortune.

- The 3rd nine, undivided: The symbol shows the subject is in a position that's similar to that of the declining sun but instead of playing an instrument and sings to it, one utters like a grumpy old man; there'll be evil.
- The 4th nine, undivided: The symbol shows the manner of the coming of one's subject. It is abrupt and to be rejected by all.

- The 5th six, divided: The symbol shows the subject as one with tears and groaning in sorrow but there'll be good fortune.

- The (uppermost) nine, undivided: The symbol shows a king employing its subject in his punitive expeditions. The subject will achieve merit for he doesn't punish prisoners; there'll be no error

Chapter Seven: Hexagrams 21 to 30

Chapter Eight: Hexagrams 31 to 40

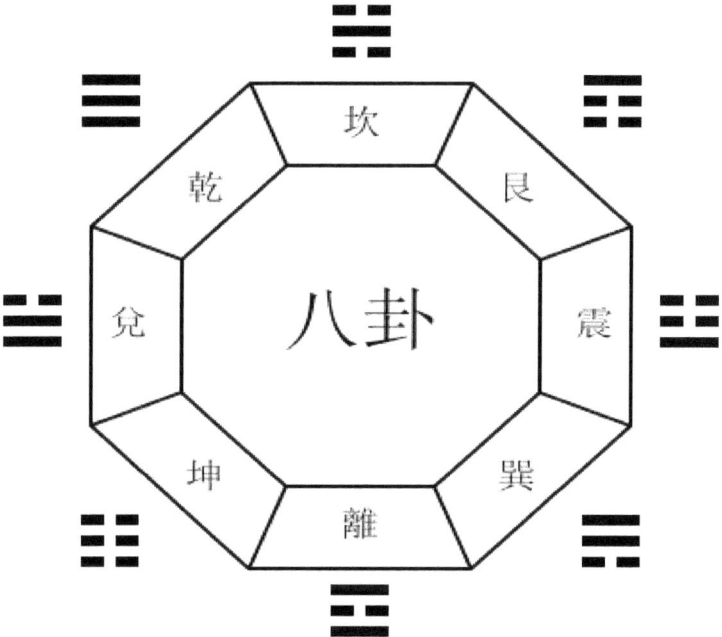

Hexagram 31: The Hsien Hexagram

Image: Lake above, Mountain below.

Attribute: Attraction.

Tranquility that's combined with excess will produce pleasure. Marriage will bring good fortune. One must accept others and be open; all changes are imminent.

Chapter Eight: Hexagrams 31 to 40

- The 1st six, divided: The symbol shows that one is moving his great toes.

- The 2nd six, divided: The symbol shows that one is moving his legs; there'll be evil but if one abides and he practiced silence, there'll be good fortune.

- The 3rd nine, undivided: The symbol shows that one is moving his thighs, and keeps close of the people he follows. If one goes forward in this way, it may likely cause regret.

- The 4th nine, undivided: The symbol shows that being firm and correct will prevent instances of repentance and will also lead to good fortune. If one is unsettled in his movements, only his friends will follow him and his purpose.

- The 5th nine, undivided: The symbol shows that one moves the flesh along the spine which is also above the heart. No repentance is required.

- The (uppermost) six, divided: The symbol shows one is moving his tongue and jaws.

Hexagram 32: The Hang Hexagram
Image: Thunder above, Wind below.
Attribute: Continuity.

The value of endurance will be taught through change and other activities. One must stand firm and be persistent to achieve a certain goal so that one will be free from committing errors.

- The 1st six, divided: The symbol shows the subject desires long continuance. Even if there's firm correctness, there'll be evil and there will be no advantage in every respect.

- The 2nd nine, undivided: The symbol shows that all occasions for repentance are disappearing.

- The 3rd nine, undivided: The symbol shows that one who doesn't continuously maintain his virtue. Some people will think of him as a disgrace and however firm he may be, there'll be occasions of regret.

- The 4th nine, undivided: The symbol shows a field where no game is taking place.

- The 5th six, divided: The symbol shows that the subject is consistently maintaining his virtue indicated by it. For a wife this shall bring good fortune but for a husband this will bring evil.

- The (uppermost) six, divided: The symbol shows that one is excited to witness the long continuance. There'll be no evil.

Hexagram 33: The Thun Hexagram
Image: Heaven above, Mountain below.
Attribute: Retreat.

The tranquil mountain remains its silence under Heaven's gaze, so does an enlightened man whenever he

Chapter Eight: Hexagrams 31 to 40

maintains dignity even in retreat. One must avoid conflict and persist only is small matters.

- The 1st six, divided: The symbol shows a retiring tail. There is a danger in this position, and no movement should be made.

- The 2nd six, divided: The symbol shows that the subject is holding his purpose of which cannot be broken.

- The 3rd nine, undivided: The symbol shows that one is retiring but bound for danger and distress but if one were to deal with his binders and nourishes a servant it will bring him good fortune.

- The 4th nine, undivided: The symbol shows the subject retiring but notwithstanding his likings. For a great man this may lead to a good fortune but an ordinary man may not attain this.

- The 5th nine, undivided: The symbol shows that the subject is retiring in an admirable way; firm correctness will bring good fortune.

- The 6th nine, undivided: The symbol shows that the subject is retiring in a noble way. This will be advantageous in every way.

Hexagram 34: The Ta Kwang Hexagram
Image: Thunder above, Heaven below.
Attribute: Power.

There is an activity to be done during the day; a wise man acts with persistence and within convention. He uses influence wisely.

- The 1st nine, undivided: The symbol shows the subject manifesting one's strength in his toes. Any advance will certainly lead to evil.

Chapter Eight: Hexagrams 31 to 40

- The 2nd nine, undivided: The symbol shows that with firm correctness there'll be good fortune.

- The 3rd nine, undivided: The symbol shows that in the case of an ordinary man, one will use all of his strength; in the case of a superior man, one whose rule is not to do so. Firmness and correctness in such position would be dangerous.

- The 4th nine, undivided: The symbol shows a case wherein firmness and correctness will lead to good fortune, and instances of repentance will disappear.

- The 5th six, divided: The symbol shows that one loses his ram or strength in the ease of his position. No repentance is required.

- The 6th six, divided: The symbol shows that one's strength is resisting against a force and is unable to retreat or advance; there'll be no advantage in every way but if one realizes the difficulty of such position, there'll be good fortune.

Hexagram 35: The Chin Hexagram
Image: Fire above, Earth below.
Attribute: Progress.

The sun rises above the earth, so does the enlightened man for he has virtues. Conditions are favorable if one pursues progress. One must help other people through one's virtues and intelligence.

- The 1st six, divided: The symbol shows that one is wishing to make an advance but retreat at the same time. If one is firm and correct, there'll be good fortune. If trust is not put in him, let him maintain a generous mind so that there'll be no mistake.

- The 2nd six, divided: The symbol shows that the subject with appears to be advancing yet it is being sorrowful. If one is firm and correct, there'll be good

Chapter Eight: Hexagrams 31 to 40

fortune and he will also receive his grandmother's blessing.

- The 3rd six, divided: The symbol shows that the subject is trusted by everyone around him. Occasions for repentance will disappear.

- The 4th nine, undivided: The symbol shows that the subject appears to be advancing but similar to a marmot. However firm or correct he may be, he is in a dangerous position.

- The 5th six, divided: The symbol shows how all occasions for repentance is gone. One must not be concern whether he will fail or succeed. If one makes an advance, he will be advantageous in every respect.

- The (uppermost) nine, undivided: The symbol shows that one is advancing his horns, but he only uses it to punish the rebels from his own city. The position is dangerous but there'll be good fortune though there'll be occasions for regret however firm or correct he may be.

Hexagram 36: The Ming I Hexagram
Image: Fire above, Earth below.
Attribute: Subtlety.

Cleverness is hidden within the earth. One must learn how to conceal goals but one must not abandon them. Conditions might be difficult but with proper persistence it will bring forth benefits.

- The 1st nine, undivided: The symbol shows that when a superior man goes away, he may not have food to eat for three days, and wherever he goes, the people will speak of him with derision.

- The 2nd six, divided: The symbol shows, as indicated in Ming I that the subject is wounded in the left thigh; he then saves himself as if he has the strength of a horse, then there'll be good fortune.

- The 3rd nine, undivided: The symbol shows, as indicated in Ming I that the subject is hunting in the south, and takes out the great chief. One should not be eager to always be correct.

- The 4th six, divided: The symbol shows the subject entered into the dark land, but one is able to carry out tasks with a clear mind.

- The 5th six, divided: The symbol shows how the count of Ki fulfilled the condition as indicated by Ming I. One would be at an advantage if one is correct and firm.

- The 6th six, divided: The symbol shows a situation where there's no light but only ambiguity. The subject ascended to the sky, and his future is to go back to the earth.

Chapter Eight: Hexagrams 31 to 40

Hexagram 37: The Kia Zan Hexagram
Image: Wind above, Fire below.
Attribute: Family.

The winds of change are issued from a clever action; an enlightened man acts in a substantial and orderly manner. One's loyalty and faith must develop.

- The 1st nine, undivided: The symbol shows that the subject establishes strict rules in his household. There'll be no instances of repentance.

- The 2nd six, divided: The symbol shows the subject is showing selflessness through attending to the preparation of food; she isn't taking anything for herself. With firm correctness, there'll be good fortune.

- The 3rd nine, undivided: The symbol shows that the subject is treating the household members with toughness. There'll be instances of repentance as well

Chapter Eight: Hexagrams 31 to 40

as perils but there'll also be good fortune. However, if the wife and children are smirking, then in the end there'll be instances for regret.

- The 4th six, divided: The symbol shows that the subject is enriching his family; there'll be good fortune.

- The 5th nine, undivided: The symbol shows the influence of the king extending to his family; there's no occasion for anxiousness, and there'll also be good fortune.

- The (uppermost) nine, undivided: The symbol shows that the subject is arrayed in royalty and possessed with sincerity. There'll be good fortune in the end.

Hexagram 38: The Khwei Hexagram
Image: Fire above, Lake below.
Attribute: Contradiction.

Intelligence contradicts excessiveness; and enlightened man only acts in small matters. One must maintain individuality.

- The 1st nine, undivided: The symbol shows that instances for repentance will disappear. One has lost his horses but he doesn't seek for them, for he knows that they will return.

- The 2nd nine, undivided: The symbol shows the subject is passing by when he met his lord. There'll be no mistake.

- The 3rd six, divided: The symbol shows that one's carriage is dragged and his oxen are also pushed. The subject is bound to shave his head and cut off his

Chapter Eight: Hexagrams 31 to 40

nose. The beginning will not be good but there'll be a good ending.

- The 4th nine, undivided: The symbol shows that the subject is alone amidst the prevailing disunion. One meets with a good man and they have a common desire. The position is dangerous but there'll be no mistake.

- The 5th six, divided: The symbol shows that the subject's instances for repentance will disappear. One unites closely with his relative and minister; there can be no error when he goes forward.

- The (uppermost) nine, undivided: The symbol shows that the subject is alone amidst the prevailing disunion. The subject who is in the third line saw a pig bearing a load of mud in its back. One bends his bow against the pig but then unbends it after awhile for the subject discovers that he's not an assailant to injure. One will meet with mild rain; there'll be good fortune.

Hexagram 39: The Kien Hexagram
Image: Water above, Mountain below.
Attribute: Obstacles.

Profundity movement meets immobility; an enlightened man perfects and studies his own behavior in order to gain strength.

- The 1st six, divided: The symbol shows that any advance from the subject will lead to more difficulties but if one remains put, he will acquire praises.

- The 2nd six, divided: The symbol shows that the minister of the king is having a hard time about the difficulties of a situation. He does not know how to perceive it and use it to his own advantage.

- The 3rd nine, undivided: The symbol shows that the subject is advancing to greater difficulties. One

Chapter Eight: Hexagrams 31 to 40

remains put and also returns to his former constituents.

- The 4th six, divided: The symbol shows that the subject is advancing to greater difficulties. One remains put and unites with his other subjects.

- The 5th nine, undivided: The symbol shows the subject is struggling with his hardships and his colleagues are coming to help him.

- The (uppermost) six, divided: The symbol shows that if the subject goes forward he will only increase his hardships, but if he stays put, he'll be more productive and also have great merit. There'll be good fortune, and one will be at an advantage of meeting great men.

Chapter Eight: Hexagrams 31 to 40

Hexagram 40: The Kieh Hexagram

Image: Thunder above, Water below.

Attribute: Liberation.

Rain and thunder denotes meaningful activity; an enlightened man will find good fortune in quick action in order to restore normal conditions. One must learn to forgive other people's faults.

- The 1st six, divided: The symbol shows that the subject will not commit any mistake.

- The 2nd nine, undivided: The symbol shows that the subject will catch three foxes and acquire yellow arrows; with correctness and firmness there'll be good fortune.

- The 3rd six, divided: The symbol shows a porter that's riding a carriage. He will tempt robbers to attack him. There'll be instances for regret if he tries to be correct and firm.

Chapter Eight: Hexagrams 31 to 40

- The 4th nine, undivided: It said, 'Remove your toes. Friends will (then) come, between you and whom there will be mutual confidence.'

- The 5th six, divided: The symbol shows the subject is a ruler or a superior man, and he is executing his function of removing any ideas that could be harmful to the idea of the hexagram. There'll be good fortune, and ordinary men will become confident of him.

- The 6th six, divided: The symbol shows that a feudal prince is trying to shoot a falcon using his bow on top of a high wall, and hitting it. There'll be an advantage in every respect as the effect of one's actions.

Chapter Eight: Hexagrams 31 to 40

Chapter Nine: Hexagrams 41 to 50

Hexagram 41: The Sun Hexagram

Image: Mountain above, Lake below.

Attribute: Decline.

Excess is held by immobility. An enlightened one must act with moderation and develop confidence. You should avoid being angry for sacrifice will bring you good fortune, and you will not commit any error.

Chapter Nine: Hexagrams 41 to 50

- The 1st nine, undivided: The symbol shows that the subject is suspending his own affairs to help the subject who is in the fourth line. One will not make any mistake but one must still consider how far he should just go when it comes to helping others.

- The 2nd nine, undivided: The symbol shows it'll be an advantage for the main subject to be consistently correct and firm, and that action on his part will be evil but he can give increase without taking from himself.

- The 3rd six, divided: The symbol shows three men walking together, and how one got lost but his friend eventually found.

- The 4th nine, divided: show its subject diminishing the pain of one of the subjects of the first line. He rushes to help him and this made him happy. There'll be no mistake.

- The 5th six, divided: The symbol shows parties added twenty pieces of tortoise shells to the store of its subject, and accepts no refusal. There'll be good fortune.

- The (uppermost) nine, undivided: The symbol shows the subject gives to others without expecting anything in return. There'll be no error, and with firm correctness there will also be good fortune. There'll be an advantage in every movement that one would make. One will also find ministers that can be counted on.

Hexagram 42: The Yi Hexagram
Image: Wind above, Thunder below,
Attribute: Benefit.

Growth brings with it great advantages. An enlightened man sees the good deeds of his companions. You should imitate them but also correct mistakes in order to achieve progress towards a certain goal.

Chapter Nine: Hexagrams 41 to 50

- The 1st nine, undivided: The symbol shows that it'll be an advantage if the subject makes a move in his position. No blame will befall him and he will receive good fortune.

- The 2nd six, divided: The symbol shows parties added twenty pieces of tortoise shells to the store of its subject whose oracles can't be opposed. Let one persevere in being correct and firm so that he will receive good fortune.

- The 3rd six, divided: The symbol shows increase given to the subjects through means of what is evil so that one shall be led to doing well and not get blamed. He must be sincere and pursue the path of the Mean.

- The 4th six, divided: The symbol represent its subject pursuing the due course. The advice that he gives to his prince is followed. He can be relied upon in such a movement as that of removing the capital.

Chapter Nine: Hexagrams 41 to 50

- The 5th nine, undivided: The symbol shows the subject with a sincere heart that seeks to benefit from the subjects below; there'll be good fortune for people will acknowledge the goodness of a sincere heart.

- The 6th nine, undivided: The symbol shows that one to whose increase none will contribute but many will try to attack him for one observes no regular rule and order in his heart. There'll be evil.

Hexagram 43: The Kwai Hexagram
Image: Lake above, Heaven below.
Attribute: Resolve.

The excess that's drawn into Heaven's gaze will produce an honest man. One must not use force but only rely on fair judgment. A man must know his goals and he should tell it to his supporters.

Chapter Nine: Hexagrams 41 to 50

- The 1st nine, undivided: The symbol shows the subject advancing with his toes because he is prideful of his strength yet he will not succeed. There'll be ground for blame.

- The 2nd nine, undivided: The symbol shows the subject is full of apprehension for help and sympathy. Hostile measures might be done against him but he doesn't need to be worried about it.

- The 3rd nine, undivided: The symbol shows the subject is about to advance with determination and a strong look on his face. There'll be evil; if the superior man walks alone, he will be hated by his colleagues as if he was contaminated by others but in the end he will not be blamed.

- The 4th nine, undivided: The symbol shows one with the skin of his bottom being stripped, and walks with difficulty. If he will learn to act like a sheep that leads after his comrades, there'll be no instances of repentance.

- The 5th nine, undivided: The symbol shows the ordinary men must be uprooted just like a bed of purslain with utmost determination. If one is determine in his actions and is in harmony with himself, there'll be no error or blame.

- The 6th six, divided: The symbol shows that the subject doesn't have any friend who he can call for help. His end will be evil.

Hexagram 44: The Kau Hexagram
Image: Heaven above, Wind below.
Attribute: Temptation.

Heaven's power makes the wind of change stronger, so too is the leader who issues commands that become well known. One must not create relationships with powerful ideas or persons. A man must show discipline.

Chapter Nine: Hexagrams 41 to 50

- The 1st nine, undivided: The symbol shows the subject should make sure that the carriage is tightly fastened to a metal drag. One must have firm correctness so that it will bring good fortune. If one moves in any direction, evil will most likely appear

- The 2nd nine, undivided: The symbol shows the subject with a wallet of fish. There'll be no mistake but it is not wise to let the subject who is in the first line to go forward to the guests.

- The 3rd nine, undivided: The symbol shows one with the skin of his bottom being stripped which is why he walks with difficulty. The position is dangerous but there'll be no great mistake.

- The 4th nine, undivided: The symbol shows the subject with his wallet but there'll be no fish in it. This will give rise to evil doings.

- The 5th nine, undivided: The symbol shows the subject as a medlar tree that's overspreading the ground under it. If one keeps his brilliant qualities hidden, a good issue will descend from Heaven.
- The 6th nine, undivided: The symbol shows that the subject received others on his horns. There'll be instances of regret but there'll be no error.

Hexagram 45: The Tsui Hexagram
Image: Lake above, Earth below.
Attribute: Assembly.

The earth receives excess. One must learn how to cooperate with others, make sacrifices and most importantly act with persistence for one to achieve a certain goal. One must act with sincerity, learn from a wise leader and try to avoid being suspicious of others.

- The 1st six, divided: The symbol shows the subject with a sincere desire for union but he is unable to carry it out which is why the chaos is brought into the sphere of his union. If he cries out, his tears will

Chapter Nine: Hexagrams 41 to 50

provide a place for his smiles. He must not mind the difficulty because it's only temporary, and as he goes forward, there'll be no mistake.

- The 2nd six, divided: The symbol shows the subject was being led forward; there'll be good fortune and there'll be no error. There is sincerity even in his small offerings.

- The 3rd six, divided: The symbol shows the subject striving after the union but cannot find any advantage. If he goes forward there could be instances of regret.

- The 4th nine, undivided: The symbol shows the subject being in the state that if he becomes very fortunate, he will not receive any blame.

- The 5th nine, undivided: The symbol shows the union of all of the subjects in the place of dignity. There'll be no error. If people don't have confidence in him, one must see to it that his virtue is firmly correct so that the need for repentance will disappear

- The (uppermost) six, divided: The symbol shows the subject weeping and sighing but there'll be no mistake.

Hexagram 46: The Shang Hexagram
Image: Earth above, Wind below.
Attribute: Advancement.

There'll be gradual change and it is nourished by the receptive earth which produces a virtuous path. An enlightened man must persist in the small matters in order to gain good fortune. One must approach leaders without fear.

- The 1st six, divided: The symbol shows the subject advancing upwards while the subject above him openly welcomes him. There'll be good fortune.

Chapter Nine: Hexagrams 41 to 50

- The 2nd nine, undivided: The symbol shows the subject with that sincerity which will make even the small sacrifices he makes acceptable. There'll be no error.

- The 3rd nine, undivided: The symbol shows the subject is ascending upwards as into an empty city.

- The 4th six, divided: The symbol shows the subject is employed by the king, and makes him present his offerings on mount Khi; there'll be good fortune and no error.

- The 5th six, divided: The symbol shows the subject being firmly correct and enjoying his good fortune. He ascends the stairs with all due ceremony.

- The (uppermost) six, divided: The symbol shows the subject advancing upwards blindly. If one maintain firm correctness, he will be advantageous in every way.

Chapter Nine: Hexagrams 41 to 50

Hexagram 47: The Khwan Hexagram

Image: Lake above, Water below.

Attribute: Adversity.

Excess that lacks profoundness. An enlightened man gains progress through his courage. Risking and experiencing adversity is needed to achieve great fortune. Speaking alone is ineffective.

- The 1st six, divided: The symbol shows the subject with his bare buttocks under the stump of a tree. He will enter a dark valley and will have no luck and deliverance for 3 years.

- The 2nd nine, undivided: The symbol shows the subject is having difficulties amidst his wine. It will be good for a man to maintain his sincerity. Active operations may lead to evil but he will not be blamed.

- The 3rd six, divided: The symbol shows the subject is straitened before a rock, he will then lay hold of the thorns before entering his palace where he won't see his wife. There'll be evil.

- The 4th nine, undivided: The symbol shows the subject is proceeding very slowly to help the subject who is in the first line. There'll be instances of regret but the end will bring good fortune.

- The 5th nine, undivided: The symbol shows the subject with his feet and nose cut off. He's straitened by the ministers who are wearing scarlet aprons. He will be leisure and satisfied with his movements.

- The (uppermost) six, divided: The symbol shows the subject is straitened as if its bound with creepers and he is in a perilous position. If he repents, there'll be good fortune as he moves forward.

Hexagram 48: The Ching Hexagram
Image: Water above, Wind below.
Attribute: Insight.

There is profound change and penetration. The truth is not exhausted yet never the same. An enlightened man will gain insight into what is true and help other people to also achieve it. If the truth isn't followed then there could be bad fortune.

- The 1st six, divided: The symbol shows a well that men will not drink out of because it is so muddy. It's an old well that even animals like birds will not drink from.

- The 2nd nine, undivided: The symbol shows a well that has a hole where water seeps out and flows to the shrimps, or water that escapes from a broken basket.

- The 3rd nine, undivided: The symbol will show a well that has been cleared out but it's not in used. If the king is intelligent, water could be drawn out and used so that the people and him can take advantage of it.

- The 4th six, divided: The symbol shows the lining of the well and how it is well – laid. There'll be no mistake.

- The 5th nine, undivided: The symbol shows a clear well where waters from cold spring are potable.

- The (uppermost) six, divided: The symbol shows the water is being brought to the top of the well. This denotes sincerity and there'll be good fortune.

Hexagram 49: The Ko Hexagram
Image: Lake above, Fire below.
Attribute: Change.

Chapter Nine: Hexagrams 41 to 50

Intelligent consciousness amid excess will produce change. An enlightened person learns from one's past experiences and presents opportunity. Confidence and progress is gained after the change has passed.

- The 1st nine, divided: The symbol shows the subject as if he were bound with the skin of a yellow ox.

- The 2nd six, divided: The symbol shows the subject making a few changes after some time has passed. Any action taken will bring good fortune. There'll be no error.

- The 3rd nine, undivided: The symbol shows that the action taken by the subject will be evil. Even if one is firm and correct, the position is dangerous. If the change that one contemplates has been fully discussed thrice, then he will be believed in.

- The 4th nine, undivided: The symbol shows that instances of repentance will disappear from the subject. Let the subject be believed in and even if he changes his existing ordinances, there'll be good fortune.

- The 5th nine, undivided: The symbol shows the great man producing his changes just like how a tiger does when he changes his stripes. Before one proceeds to action, faith has already been reposed in him.

- The (uppermost) six, divided: The symbol shows the superior man producing his changes just like how a leopard does when it changes its spots, while ordinary men show obedience and also change their faces. To go advance now would lead to evil but if one is firm and correct will meet good fortune.

Hexagram 50: The Ting Hexagram
Image: Fire above, Wind below.
Attribute: Order.

Chapter Nine: Hexagrams 41 to 50

Intelligence in combination with penetration will create good fortune and make progress. A wise man aligns himself with an established order.

- The 1st six, divided: The symbol shows a caldron has its feet turned up and overthrown but there'll be an advantage if one gets rid of what is bad in it. There'll be no mistake.

- The 2nd nine, undivided: The symbol shows a caldron with things being cooked inside of it. There'll be good fortune.

- The 3rd nine, undivided: The symbol shows the caldron with its ears changed. The progress of a subject is thus stopped. The fat flesh that's being cooked in the caldron won't be eaten. The instances for repentance will be gone; in the end, there'll good fortune.

- The 4th nine, undivided: The symbol shows that a caldron has its feet broken. The contents of the

Chapter Nine: Hexagrams 41 to 50

caldron that's designed for the leader is overturned. There'll be evil and the ruler's subject will be shamed.

- The 5th six, divided: The symbol shows that a caldron has rings of metal and has yellow ears but there'll be advantage by being correct and firm.

- The 6th nine, undivided: The symbol shows a caldron has rings of jade. There'll be good fortune and all advances will be advantageous in every respect

Chapter Ten: Hexagrams 51 to 64

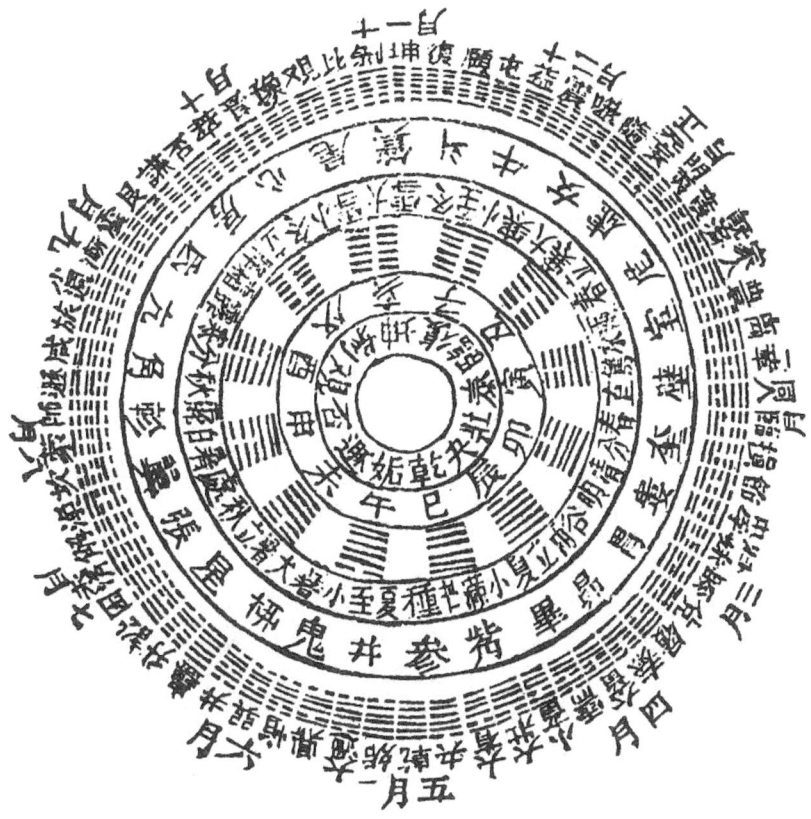

Hexagram 51: The Kan Hexagram

Image: Thunder above, Thunder below.

Attribute: Shock.

Repeated activity will produce fear and surprise; an enlighten man seeks to improve himself and finds a way to make the unpredictable beneficial for him.

- The 1st nine, undivided: The symbol shows that when the movement begins to approach, the subject will look around with apprehension. He will then talk cheerfully and smile, there'll be good fortune.

- The 2nd six, divided: The symbol shows that when the movement begins, the subject will be in a dangerous position. He will need to make a choice to let go of his possessions so that he can move swiftly; he will find his items in 7 days.

- The 3rd six, divided: The symbol shows that the subject is distraught even if there are startling movements. If such movements excite him, he will act right and there'll be no mistake.

- The 4th nine, undivided: The symbol shows that the subject will sink deeper in the mud in the middle of the startling movements.

- The 5th six, divided: The symbol shows that the subject is going and coming amidst the startling movements, and he will always be in danger. He will not incur any loss and may find a task that he needs to accomplish.

- The (uppermost) six, divided: The symbol shows the subject is in breathless dismay amidst the startling movements. He is looking around with trembling apprehension. If one takes action, there'll be evil. If the startling movements haven't yet reached him or his neighborhood, there'll be no error if he were to take precautionary measures but his relatives may speak against him.

Hexagram 52: The Kan Hexagram
Image: Mountain above, Mountain below.
Attribute: Meditation.

Tranquility upon tranquility; and enlightened man turns his back upon a difficult situation and loses self – awareness. If one doesn't notice anyone else, there's no error.

- The 1st six, divided: The symbol shows that the subject keeps his toes at rest. There'll be no error but he can take advantage if he is consistently firm, correct and persistent.

- The 2nd six, divided: The symbol shows that the subject is keeping the back of his legs at rest. He will not be able to help others and he will feel dissatisfied in his mind.

- The 3rd nine, undivided: The symbol shows the subject keeping his loins at rest. The position he is in is dangerous but the heart glows with suppressed excitement.

- The 4th six, divided: The symbol shows that the subject keeps his trunk at rest. There'll be no mistake.

- The 5th six, divided: The symbol shows that the subject keeps his jawbones at rest and that his words are orderly. The instances for repentance will be gone.

- The 6th nine, undivided: The symbol shows the subject maintain his restful state. There'll be good fortune.

Hexagram 53: The Kien Hexagram
Image: Wind above, Mountain below.
Attribute: Development.

Penetrating change moves the immovable mountain. An enlightened person improves his life by being persistent and maintaining good conduct. Marriage brings good fortune.

- The 1st six, divided: The symbol shows a wild goose slowly approaching the shorelines. A young officer will be in a perilous position; others will speak against him but there'll be no error.

- The 2nd six, divided: The symbol shows that the goose is slowly approaching over large rocks where it will eat and drink while being at ease. There'll be good fortune.

- The 3rd nine, undivided: The symbol shows the goose is slowly advancing to the dry plains. It also suggests the idea of a husband who is going to an expedition from which he will never return to his wife who is pregnant with their child. There'll be evil.

- The 4th six, divided: The symbol shows that the good slowly goes to the trees. They will lie on the branches, and there'll be no error.

- The 5th nine, undivided: The symbol shows that the goose slowly goes to the high mound. This suggests the idea that a wife for three years doesn't become pregnant but in the end this natural circumstance can't be avoided. There'll still be good fortune.

- The 6th nine, undivided: The symbol shows that the goose slowly goes to the large heights. The feathers can be used as ornaments. There'll be good fortune.

Hexagram 54: The Kwei Mei Hexagram

Image: Thunder above, Lake below.

Attribute: Passivity.

Action above, and excess below. An enlightened man who is suffering will take no action but will still consider the near future. One must seek no goal.

- The 1st nine, undivided: The symbol shows the younger sister being married off in a position ancillary to the real wife. It denotes the idea of a person who can only stand on one leg yet still manages to move along. Going forward will bring good fortune.

- The 2nd nine, undivided: The symbol shows that the wife is blind in one eye but she is still able to see. There'll be an advantage if she is to maintain her firmness as a solitary widow.

- The 3rd six, divided: The symbol shows the younger sister was to be married off in a mean position. She will return and accept an ancillary position.

- The 4th nine, undivided: The symbol shows that the younger sister who is to be married off is protracting time. She will be late in getting married but the time will come.

- The 5th six, divided: The symbol suggests that the thought of the full moon will bring good fortune.

- The 6th six, divided: The symbol shows a young lady bearing the basket but it doesn't have anything on it, there's also a gentleman slaughtering a sheep but there's no blood flowing from it. There'll be no advantage in every respect.

Hexagram 55: The Fang Hexagram

Image: Thunder above, Fire below.

Attribute: Peaking intelligence.

Intelligence that's combined with activity is the zenith of success. An enlightened person knows how to trust his/her own judgment and make progress.

- The 1st nine, undivided: The symbol shows the subject is meeting with his mate. They are of the same character and there'll be no error.

- The 2nd six, divided: The symbol shows that the subject is surrounded by large and thick screens. If he go and tries to enlighten his leader, he will look suspicious. Let him cherish his feeling of sincere devotion so that he can move his leader's mind and bring good fortune.

- The 3rd nine, undivided: The symbol shows that the subject has an additional screen of a large and thick banner. There'll be no error.

- The 4th nine, undivided: The symbol shows that the subject is inside a large and thick tent in the middle of the day. He will meet a subject from the first line who is undivided like himself. There'll be good fortune.

- The 5th six, divided: The symbol shows the subject is surrounded by intellectual men. There'll be occasion for praises and congratulations. There will also be good fortune.

- The uppermost six, divided: The symbol shows the subject has a large house and as he looks inside there's nobody in it. For three years no one lives there. There'll be evil.

Hexagram 56: The Lu Hexagram
Image: Fire above, Mountain below.
Attribute: Travel.

Illumination upon the silent mountain creates favorable conditions for travel. A wise man has a clear mind and is not detained by any disputes.

- The 1st six, divided: The symbol shows the stranger mean as well as the meanly occupied thus it brings on a man further calamity.

- The 2nd six, divided: The symbol shows a stranger living in a lodging – house and carries with him the means of livelihood. He is with good and trustworthy servants.

- The 3rd nine, undivided: The symbol shows the stranger burning his lodging – house and have lost his servants. However one is correct and firm, he will be in danger.

- The 4th nine, undivided: The symbol shows a traveler in a resting place while having a means of livelihood and axe but one still says, 'I'm not at ease in my mind.'

- The 5th six, divided: The symbol shows the subject shooting a peasant. The subject will lose his arrow but in the end he will get a praise and a high charge

- The 6th nine, undivided: The symbol suggests the idea of a burn burning its own nest. A stranger first laughs before crying out, he will also lose his ox easily and there'll be evil.

Hexagram 57: The Sun Hexagram
Image: Wind above, Wind below.
Attribute: Influence.

Penetrating change above and below; an enlightened man acts in a gradual way and only towards small goals. One must patiently wait and also consider bigger perspectives.

- The 1st six, divided: The symbol shows that a subject is advancing now and also receding now. It'll be an advantage for one if he has a firm correctness as that of a brave soldier.

- The 2nd nine, undivided: The symbol shows the representative of Sun under a couch, and hiring diviners and exorcists in such a way of bordering on confusion. There'll be good fortune and no mistake.

- The 3rd nine, undivided: The symbol shows that the subject is penetrating only through violent and repeated efforts. There'll be instances for regret.

- The 4th six, divided: The symbol shows all instances for repentance in its subject. One takes a game for 3 – fold use in one's hunting.

- The 5th nine, undivided: The symbol shows that with firm correctness, there'll be good fortune to the subject. All instances for repentance will be gone, and all of the subject's movements will be advantageous. There may have been no good start but there'll be a good finish. Three days before making any changes let him give notice to them, and let him reconsider them after 3 days. There'll be good fortune.

- The 6th nine, undivided: The symbol a representative of penetration under a couch, and having lost one's axe with which one uses to execute decisions. However firm and correct one will try to be, there'll be evil.

Hexagram 58: The Tui Hexagram
Image: Lake above, Lake below.
Attribute: Encouragement.

Openness and excess above and below, a wise man knows how to exchange ideas with other people in order to find cooperation among them. Correct persistence will result to progress and also an advantage.

- The 1st nine, undivided: The symbol shows the pleasure of one's inward harmony. There'll be good fortune.

- The 2nd nine, undivided: The symbol shows the pleasure arising from one's inward sincerity. Instances for repentance will be gone, and there'll be good fortune.

- The 3rd six, divided: The symbol shows that the subject is bringing unto himself whatever can give him pleasure. There'll be evil.

- The 4th nine, undivided: The symbol shows the subject is deliberating about what he must seek his pleasure in and not at rest. One borders on what will cause injury but there'll be causes for joy.

- The 5th nine, undivided: The symbol shows that a subject is putting his trust unto someone who will harm him. The situation is dangerous.

- The (uppermost) six, divided: The symbol shows the pleasure of the subject that draws and leads others.

Hexagram 59: The Hwan Hexagram
Image: Wind above, Water below.
Attribute: Reunion.

Gradual change above profound water; rulers will meet with their subordinates. There'll be advantage if one learns how to cooperate and do so with correct persistence.

- The 1ˢᵗ six, divided: The symbol shows the subject is engaged in rescuing someone from impending evil. One will have the assistance of a strong horse, and there'll be good fortune.

- The 2ⁿᵈ nine, undivided: The symbol shows the subject amidst the dispersion will hurry to his contrivance to become secure. Instances for repentance will be gone.

- The 3ʳᵈ six, divided: The symbol shows that the subject is discarding any regard to his own self. There'll be no instances for repentance.

- The 4ᵗʰ six, divided: The symbol shows the subject scattering different parties which will lead to good fortune. From the dispersion, one collects good men which ordinary men wouldn't have thought of.

- The 5ᵗʰ nine, undivided: The symbol shows the subject amidst the dispersion issuing announcements as his body perspires. He scatters the accumulation in royal granaries. There'll be no mistake.

- The (uppermost) nine, undivided: The symbol shows the subject disposing of what is called bloody wounds. He will go and separate himself from its anxious fears. There'll be no mistake.

Hexagram 60: The Kieh Hexagram
Image: Lake below, Water above.
Attribute: Limitation.

Profoundness is held in check by excess. A wise person must learn how to develop sound restraints and knows how to decide proper conduct. There is no virtue in extreme limitation.

- The 1st nine, undivided: The symbol shows the subject is not quitting the courtyard that is outside his door. There'll be no mistake.

- The 2nd nine, undivided: The symbol shows the subject is not quitting the courtyard inside his gate. There'll be evil.

- The 3rd six, divided: The symbol shows the subject with no appearance of observing proper guidelines, in which case, we will see him lamenting. There will be no one to blame but himself.

- The 4th six, divided: The symbol shows the subject is naturally and silently attentive to all the guidelines. There'll be success and progress.

- The 5th nine, undivided: The symbol shows the subject sweetly enacts his regulations. There'll be good fortune and the onward progress will be grounds for admiration.

- The (uppermost) six, divided: The symbol shows the subject enacting regulations that are hard and severe. However firm and correct he may be, there'll be evil but the instances of repentance will by and by be gone.

Hexagram 61: The Kung Fu Hexagram
Image: Wind above, Lake below.
Attribute: Understanding.

Penetrating change above the open lake, from a distance, a wise man gains clarity and understanding. There are only moderate disputes and one should avoid rigidity.

- The 1st nine, undivided: The symbol shows the subject is resting in himself; there'll be good fortune. If he sought to other things, he wouldn't find rest

- The 2nd nine, undivided: The symbol shows the subject appears to be crane crying out in her hidden retirement.

- The 3rd six, divided: The symbol shows the subject having met his mate. Now one beats his drum and left off. Now, he weeps and also sings.

- The 4th six, divided: The symbol shows the subject like a nearly full moon and a horse in a chariot whose companion disappears. There'll be no mistake.

- The 5th nine, undivided: The symbol shows the subject is very much sincere to him in closest union. There'll be no error.

- The (uppermost) nine, undivided: The symbol shows the subject in chanticleer who's trying to mount to heaven. There'll be evil even if one is firm and correct.

Hexagram 62: The Hsiao Kwo Hexagram
Image: Thunder above, Mountain below,
Attribute: Attention to detail.

As the mountain remains at peace in activity, so is the wise man. He knows how to conduct himself with control and dignity. He is remorseful in losses and also frugal when it comes to expenses.

- The 1st six, divided: The symbol suggests the idea of a bird ascending above until the issue is evil.

- The 2nd six, divided: The symbol shows the subject passing by his grandpa and also meeting with his grandma; he does not attempt anything against his leader, but meeting him as his minister. There'll be no mistake.

- The 3rd nine, undivided: The symbol shows the subject taking no precautionary measures against danger. Others will find an opportunity to attack him. There'll be evil.

- The 4th nine, undivided: The symbol shows the subject falling into no error. However, if he goes forward, there could be danger therefore he must be cautious. There's no instance to be using firmness perpetually.

- The 5th six, divided: The symbol suggests the idea of dense clouds with no rain that comes from the western border. It also portrays a prince shooting his arrow and striking a bird that is in a cave.

- The 6th six, divided: The symbol shows the subject not meeting the exigency of his situation and also exceeding his proper course. It also suggests the idea of a bird flying far aloft; there'll be evil. It is a self – produced injury.

Hexagram 63: The Ki Chi Hexagram
Image: Water above, Fire below.
Attribute: Precaution.

In consciousness is bred profound difficulty. An enlightened man knows how to defend himself against forthcoming adversities. Confusion is imminent and there will only be progress in small matters.

- The 1st nine, undivided: The symbol shows the subject as a driver who drags his wheel. It is also similar to a fox that drags his wet tail. There'll be no mistake.

- The 2nd six, divided: The symbol shows that a wife has long her carriage, one need not to go after it for in 7 days she will find it.

- The 3rd nine, undivided: The symbol suggests the case of Kao Chung who was attacked by the Demon region but took 3 years in subduing it. Ordinary men shouldn't be employed in such enterprises.

- The 4th six, divided: The symbol shows the subject has provided rags in order to stop his boat from leaking. He is guarding it all day long.

- The 5th nine, undivided: The symbol shows the subject as the neighbor in the east who kills an ox as a sacrifice but this isn't equal to the small sacrifice of the neighbor from the west whose sincerity receives the blessing.

- The (uppermost) six, divided: The symbol shows the subject with his head immersed. The position is dangerous.

Hexagram 64: The Wei Chi Hexagram

Image: Fire above, Water below.

Attribute: Vigilance.

Consciousness above the difficult water; a wise man attends his position and carefully makes progress. One progresses but with great vigilance.

- The 1st six, divided: The symbol shows the subject similar to a fox whose tail get immersed. There'll be instances for regret.

- The 2nd nine, undivided: The symbol shows the subject is dragging back its carriage. If one is correct and firm, there'll be good fortune.

- The 3rd six, divided: The symbol shows the subject with things that aren't yet remedied. If one advances on, it will lead to evil.

- The 4th nine, undivided: The symbol shows the subject maintains his firmness and correctness; this will bring good fortune and instances for repentance will be gone.

- The 5th six, divided: The symbol shows the subject maintains his firmness and correctness; this will bring good fortune and instances for repentance will be gone. We see the subject possessing sincerity and the brightness of a superior man. There'll be good fortune.

- The (uppermost) nine, undivided: The symbol shows the subject is full of confidence and is silently feasting. There'll be no error. If one cherish such confidence just like a fox that gets his head immersed, it'll fail of what is right.

Conclusion

The I Ching represents an entire ancient philosophy which is why it should be treated with great respect as it symbolizes the interconnectedness of the universe and the cycle of life. It also serves as a moral guide so that individuals can find their own course and achieve balance and harmony. The wisdom that the Book of Changes contains can potentially stimulate one's creativity, resourcefulness, and sensitivity; this ancient divination system will help you deal with everyday challenges in your life so that you can make better decisions and achieve a more desirable or favorable outcome but most importantly it empowers and encourages an individual or a seeker to look inside oneself in order to find the answer that a person seeks.

The I Ching or the Book of Changes is a global literature treasure that is beloved by many intellectuals from both the east and the west, and it has also been used and recommended by many influential people in the past and of today but just like any other divination system, the truth already lies within you, you must learn to look within yourself for it already knows the answer to what you seek.

Photo Credits

Introduction Page Photo by Glitchwitch user via pixabay.com,

https://pixabay.com/en/i-ching-bagua-trigram-feng-2147503/

Page 2 Photo by user Natasha G via pixabay.com, https://pixabay.com/en/luck-coins-lucky-coins-662036/

Page 10 Photo by user Sarah Altendorf via flickr.com, https://www.flickr.com/photos/sarah_elizabeth_simpson/5988994785/

Page 18 Photo by user V.T. Polywoda via flickr.com, https://www.flickr.com/photos/vtpoly/15770331798/

Page 25 Photo by user Amber Case via flickr.com, https://www.flickr.com/photos/caseorganic/7744795444/

Page 31 Photo taken from The Yi Jing, or Book of Changes: A Very Brief Overview via Indiana University, Early Chinese Thought [B/E/P374]

http://www.indiana.edu/~p374/Yijing.pdf

Page 51 Photo taken from The Yi Jing, or Book of Changes: A Very Brief Overview via Indiana University, Early Chinese Thought [B/E/P374]

http://www.indiana.edu/~p374/Yijing.pdf

Page 69 Photo taken from The Yi Jing, or Book of Changes: A Very Brief Overview via Indiana University, Early Chinese Thought [B/E/P374]

http://www.indiana.edu/~p374/Yijing.pdf

Page 87 Photo by user Manuel Strehl viaWikimedia.org,

https://commons.wikimedia.org/wiki/File:Acht-trigramme.svg

Page 106 Photo by user thierry ehrmann via flickr.com,

https://www.flickr.com/photos/home_of_chaos/3928480577/

Page 126 Photo taken from The Yi Jing, or Book of Changes: A Very Brief Overview via Indiana University, Early Chinese Thought [B/E/P374]

http://www.indiana.edu/~p374/Yijing.pdf

References

I Ching Reading: A Step-by-Step Guide – Exemplore.com
https://exemplore.com/fortune-divination/I_Ching_divination

How to Use I Ching Hexagrams – LovetoKnow.com
https://feng-shui.lovetoknow.com/yin-yang/i-ching-hexagrams

The I Ching – Biroco.com
https://www.biroco.com/yijing/Legge1899.pdf

I Ching: The Book of Changes - Labirintoermetico.com
http://www.labirintoermetico.com/09iching/cleary_thomas_the_taoist_i_ching.pdf

The Tao of the I Ching – MagicHypercubes.com
http://www.magichypercubes.com/Encyclopedia/i/IChingPaper.pdf

Introduction of I Ching – Iging.com
https://www.iging.com/intro/introduc.htm

How to Consult the I Ching - Divination.com
https://divination.com/how-to-consult-the-i-ching/

Introduction to the I Ching – EclecticEnergies.com
https://www.eclecticenergies.com/iching/introduction

www.ingramcontent.com/pod-product-compliance
Lightning Source LLC
LaVergne TN
LVHW051835080426
835512LV00018B/2892